UNDER PRESSURE

SINGLES ▲ A SERIES EDITED BY JOSHUA CLOVER AND EMILY J. LORDI

UNDER PRESSURE

MAX BRZEZINSKI

DUKE UNIVERSITY PRESS DURHAM AND LONDON 2025

© 2025 Duke University Press

All rights reserved

Printed in the United States of America on acid-free paper ∞

Project Editor: Lisa Lawley

Designed by Matthew Tauch

Typeset in Bitter and Work Sans by Copperline Book Services

Library of Congress Cataloging-in-Publication Data

Names: Brzezinski, Max, author.

Title: Under pressure : a song by David Bowie and Queen /
Max Brzezinski.

Other titles: Singles (Duke University Press)

Description: Durham : Duke University Press, 2025. | Series:
Singles | Includes bibliographical references and index.

Identifiers: LCCN 2024022131 (print)

LCCN 2024022132 (ebook)

ISBN 9781478031192 (paperback)

ISBN 9781478026976 (hardcover)

ISBN 9781478060192 (ebook)

Subjects: LCSH: Bowie, David — Criticism and interpretation. |
Queen (Musical group). Under pressure. | Queen (Musical
group) — Criticism and interpretation. | Rock music —
1981 – 1990 — History and criticism. | Popular music —
1981 – 1990 — History and criticism. | Popular music — Social
aspects. | Popular music — Political aspects.

Classification: LCC ML421.Q44 B78 2025 (print) |
LCC ML421.Q44 (ebook) | DDC 782.42166092/2 — dc23/eng/20240515

LC record available at https://lccn.loc.gov/2024022131

LC ebook record available at https://lccn.loc.gov/2024022132

CONTENTS

⏸ Intro
Anthem, Counter-Anthem, Anthemic

IN THE FALL OF 1977, Queen and David Bowie each released singles destined to become anthems: on September 23, Bowie released "'Heroes'"; two weeks later, Queen dropped "We Are the Champions" with "We Will Rock You" on the flip side. "'Heroes,'" although put out in German, French, and English editions, was only a minor chart success. Both sides of Queen's 45 were immediate smashes.

Queen wrote "We Are the Champions" and "We Will Rock You" with mass consumption, arenas, and stadiums in mind. Both were reverse engineered from a live show in May 1977 during which a rowdy audience stamped, clapped, and sang Liverpool FC's anthem "You'll Never Walk Alone." Soon after, Queen created a 45 that channeled crowd behavior and expectation into a perfect pop commodity. Demographic market research here preceded artistic inspiration: "I was thinking about football when I wrote it," Freddie Mercury recalled of "We Are the Champions."[1] Market research, then, but also applied physics: Brian May recorded the memorable percussion of "We Will Rock You" at various distances, "all prime numbers" apart, "so you just feel like you're in the middle of a large number of people stamping on boards and clapping."[2]

Both songs are lyrically skeletal, almost contentless. The lyrics do nothing more than reiterate the music's effects: we will rock you, we are the champions. These minimal, self-contained songs are universal machines, inventions intended to produce direct and monumental affect in large crowds and simulate it for the home listener.

Queen's combination of rousing technical effects with place-holder lyrical forms was intentional. As Roger Taylor recently said of his band's relation to commitment: "In Queen, we always tried to be apolitical," while May once noted that "[a] Queen audience is a football crowd which doesn't take sides."[3] In Queen's anthems, banners are waved "all over all the place," but the combatants and stakes are unclear. "We Are the Champions" auto-allegorizes Queen's attempt to become stars but is open-ended enough that any listener can number themselves among the *we*. "We Will Rock You" focalizes the rocker, not the rocked. They were written to empower crowds of all types, no matter the political, economic, and social divisions within them.

Bowie's "'Heroes,'" a song of furtive love under the shadows of the Berlin Wall, gathered its popularity more slowly than Queen's contemporaneous release. The power of "'Heroes'" initially seemed a different sort than Queen's: It's not musically direct or lyrically neutralized enough to be a jock jam. It's a dark, ambivalent song about alcoholic, erotic, and geopolitical tumult — not a monumental song of triumph. Built on Robert Fripp's woozy, interval-jumping guitar eruptions and a volume-dependent microphone rig that applied different effects on Bowie's voice depending on its amplitude, the track is a counter-anthem for outsiders struggling under the oppressive weight of Cold War terror. It takes sides, and only underdogs can really identify with it. Bowie scare-quoted the title of "'Heroes'" (both the song and its album) to emphasize that melodramas of heroes and villains were beside the point. The anthem crosses out the possibility of heroism and victory for a period any longer than "just for one day." The only thing it insists upon is struggle, and only for survival levels of meaning and connection.

By 1977, then, pop musicians like Queen and Bowie were taking up the mantle of exhausted institutional anthems in opposed, contradictory fashions. But "We Are the Champions," "We Will Rock You," and "'Heroes'" alike announced that national airs, church sing-alongs, and revolutionary hymns were tapped out, even embarrassing. Such "classic" anthems no longer inspired and fused communal imaginaries like the "wretched of the earth" of the nation, the church flock, or "The Internationale."

Whether ultranationalist, ecclesiastical, or radical, these traditional songs' propagandistic power to train and move citizens, parishioners, and believers was rapidly diminishing. Red Krayola's Mayo Thompson's 1981 put-down of "The Internationale" as "inflated and overwrought" held more generally for the historical condition of lesser anthems of church and state.[4] Even true believers could only pay lip service to the sense of the old airs while no longer feeling the music: a case more of inertial obligation than aesthetic passion. In the era of structural adjustment and deindustrialization, self-consciously grand anthems like "The Battle Hymn of the Republic," "Deutschland Über Alles," "The Sacred War," and "Ode to Joy" (retrofitted as the EU's "Anthem of Europe") were now productions of an inaccessible, pre-45 era, with limited aesthetic and political purchase on the present. By the late 1970s, all institutions that formerly inspired collective belonging seemed corrupted—the wars nation-states waged were dirty and antiheroic, democracy and communism had both suffered elite capture by bureaucrats and kleptocrats, and corporations were busy rediscovering their passion for outsourcing and sweatshops. Grassroots countermovements were either AstroTurfed from the outset or harassed and tortured out of existence.

The only ascendant collectives with a hopeful future seemed to be members of antidemocratic institutions, nominally national but increasingly globalized: businesspeople, spies, paramilitaries, and lobbyists. The cohesion between these players is better described as authoritarian solidarity than revolutionary camaraderie, given that their shared goals were to jack up oil prices and control wages, overthrow leftists and social democrats at home and abroad, jockey for neo-imperial preeminence, and maintain bottom lines and monopolies of violence.

As a result, long gone were the days in which anthems inspired true fervor, or even genuine crises of political conscience. C. L. R. James gives a sense of this dissonance between the anthem as a form and the content it might be called upon to convey. In *The Black Jacobins*, James relates a story of French legionnaires in 1802 shocked to hear Haitian rebels singing "their" anthems of freedom: "Yet at nights they heard the blacks in the fortress singing the *Marseillaise*, the Ça Ira, and the other revolutionary songs. Lacroix records how these misguided wretches as they heard the songs started and looked at the officers as if to say, 'Have our barbarous enemies justice on their side? Are we no longer the soldiers of Republican France? And have we become the crude instruments of policy?'"[5] By the 1970s, it seems all sides felt like crude instruments of policy. The reasons for a newer phase of crisis in the traditional anthem form were multiple and over-determined. I count three major ones:

1 Traditional anthems of state, church, and revolutionary movements had aged poorly compared to the productions of the cultural industry. The sonics of the older anthems felt dated to contemporary listeners, even those committed to their ideological contents.
2 Older airs' grandiosity of address to entire nations, large congregations, international masses, and global diasporas no longer accorded with the grimmer, more fragmented, and contradiction-riven realities of collective life after World War II, and especially post-1968 and what Eric Hobsbawm has called the "crisis decades."[6]
3 A century of total war and global capitalist expansion had ravaged the local and national institutions whose spirit these anthems previously incarnated and promulgated. The old anthems were flagging in strength as the aesthetic, social, and political terrain underneath them gave way, but the hunger for new ones remained sharp and keening.

Enter the pop anthem. In supplanting the older anthems in content, many new strains of pop music anthem in the decade before 1981 and "Under Pressure" retrofitted and transformed their essential formal lineaments for new uses. Whether travestied, inverted, or pastiched, underground or corporate, the welter of new popular anthems released between 1968 and 1981 had to maintain some connection to tradition to remain legible and successful.

So the new anthemics continued to draw out intense bodily and emotional participation from listeners — if not in the footstomps and war-whoops of Queen's arena rock fans, then in the humming, dancing, miming, and singing-along of bedroom dwellers and drivers. The new pop anthems aimed to *move* people, both in a literal, physical sense and in an internal, subjective, affective one. They still articulated at least an attenuated collective vision — they were "we" songs, not singer-songwriter confessions. Most of the new pop anthems, unlike Queen, still named an enemy.

Pop anthems, like their nationalist, religious, and internationalist predecessors, were still, at least nominally, songs of struggle. As a result, they needed to map out their contemporary historical conjecture, in both sound and lyric. They approached this task of diagnostic analysis — sketching the shape of their present moment — to lay out a vision of an improved, optative, or even utopian state. All this they had to do, as of old, in grand, heightened style. Furthermore, as anthems are, by definition, melodramatic allegories of the collective's relation to institutions, these newer anthems, like the old ones, required a capacious view on human affairs and a monumental, even epic tone. Of course, a pop song could possess all these qualities and still fail to be legitimated as an anthem by mass audiences.

The pop anthem is an index of social bondedness and, partially, its producer. The anthem is a form that represents the contemporary state of collective relation; it is also something that offers the musical means to invent new collective states, conjuring fresh groupings by creating new affects or feelings and, as Gilles Deleuze and Félix Guattari observed, "mak[e] us become with them."[7] In daily life, we still tend to separate the domain of representation, thought, and language from that of affect. Against this false partition that would separate the ideas in a song from its sentiments, in pop music they run in parallel, intertwine, or contradict but never separate.

This combination of analytical, narrative diagnoses of the present and its capacity to help invent future affects makes pop music inherently unstable: it works differently in every song. But unlike loner singer-songwriting or dyadic love songs, the pop anthem must keep faith with group subjects and experiments in collective feeling.

But what collectives could still be depicted and promoted in the 1970s? The desire for the anthem, for belief, belonging, and a cause, was seemingly objectless. By the time the seventies were in full swing, no existing institutions seemed likely bearers of a more egalitarian, progressive, let alone revolutionary, future. The Nitty Gritty Dirt Band's sanguine 1971 answer to the question "Will the circle be unbroken?" on their cover for an album of the same name — that "music forms a new circle" — in its vaporous modesty beat quite a retreat from more radical forms of utopianism.

And by the mid- to late seventies, all forms of collective possibility seemed shut down. The dreams of Marxism-Leninism were bogged down by Soviet bureaucratic malaise and declining rates of economic growth; in the years before his death in 1976, Mao had lost the plot and loosed the furies of the Cultural Revolution on the Chinese citizenry; in foreign policy, the United States remained committed to providing cash, guns, soldiers, and the CIA to any reactionary in Africa and the Americas willing to kill leftists, while mass bombing civilians in Vietnam, Laos, and Cambodia; OPEC tormented Western nations, manipulating prices to produce not one but two oil crises. Suffering economically, Labour in the UK proved an ineffectual guardian of workers and immigrants and inflamed conflicts with the IRA into widespread violence.

Meanwhile, profit-seeking corporations found they could more effectively exploit workers by moving factories to global zones of underdevelopment. As the decade ended, a rare double-dip recession paired rampant inflation with rising unemployment. Ronald Reagan, Margaret Thatcher, full-financialization, and renewed threats of nuclear war were in the air. Godfrey Reggio's end card for *Koyaanisqatsi* featured a series of definitions of the Hopi word that provides the 1982 movie's title:

1   crazy life.
2   life in turmoil.
3   life out of balance.
4   life disintegrating.
5   a state of life that calls for another way of living.[8]

This concisely captures the affective dimensions of the dead-locked times. As to where or how to bring into being this other way of living, no one was quite sure. Margarethe von Trotta's 1981 masterpiece *Die bleierne Zeit* allegorizes only the dead end, through the tale of two sisters, one revolutionary, one liberal. At the film's end, Marianne the radical terrorist has been murdered by the state in prison, and her sister, feminist journalist Juliane, can't convince any papers to even investigate Marianne's killing.

Such unpropitious times demanded new anthems. But ironically, these same times so troubled the traditional economic, political, and affective conditions of possibility for the creation of such anthems that the culture industry seemed at a loss. What could be done?

Amedeo D'Adamo claims new pop anthems became "critical," by which he means they sought to redeem an abandoned American democratic spirit via constructive criticism: his central example is, oddly, the Anti-American camp of "Young Americans."[9] D'Adamo locates this spirit in everything from Woody Guthrie to Beyoncé's cover of "At Last" for the Obamas. But it is unclear whether Guthrie's America is Beyoncé's or whether all pop anthems ever did or ever ought to launder the reputation of the US empire, whether in liberal or reactionary terms.

So just rebranding nationalism as critical won't hack it. In fact, between the late sixties and the early eighties, pop music anthems splintered and proliferated in manifold directions. There were not only critical anthems but counter-anthems, national collapse anthems, internationalist anthems, subcultural anthems, pure pop antipolitical anthems, and anti-anthems. Some were nihilistic, some utopian, some intended for small DIY communities, some for the unrestricted transnationalism of major label or diasporic distribution, some a flight from the anthem altogether, born out of the same spirit that inspired Donald Fagen to profess that "anthemic rock music is inherently fascist — anything intended to move huge masses of people is politically offensive to me."[10] These multifarious forms were often politically and aesthetically opposed to one another, and even had contradictory expressions in style and substance, and so cannot be too hastily lumped together. The present book articulates the form's politics and poetics, with "Under Pressure" representing both its culmination and inflection point.

To begin with, the late sixties/early seventies churned with counter-anthems: these critiqued nationalism, militarism, and moralism and expressed the hope that the youth culture could imagine and manifest an alternative nation. And in negative mode, Jimi Hendrix's famous rendition of "The Star-Spangled Banner" at Woodstock stripped the anthem of its traditional, ideological lyrics and interpolated the sounds of machine gun fire, screams, and wails into the anthem. The song called on the crowd at 1969's Woodstock to demolish the old national culture and build an entirely new society. Jazz bassist Charlie Haden described a similar scene in the notes to *Liberation Music Orchestra* (1969), in which anti-Vietnam delegates sang "We Shall Overcome" at the 1968 Democratic National Convention in Chicago: "Unable to gain control of the floor, the rostrum instructed the convention orchestra to drown out the singing. 'You're a Grand Old Flag' and 'Happy Days Are Here Again' could then be heard trying to stifle 'We Shall Overcome.'" On the album bearing these notes, Haden and his band of out-jazz all-stars extended the idea, offering versions of Spanish Republican partisan and workers' songs, civil rights anthems, and an ode to Che Guevara to help listeners "creat[e] a better world, a world without war and killing, without racism, without poverty and exploitation."[11]

In the UK, the distance traveled from Bowie's "Changes" (written and recorded in 1971) to "All the Young Dudes" (written and demoed by Bowie, given to Mott the Hoople in 1972) represents the speed at which history was moving. In "Changes," Bowie had proclaimed that the "children . . . trying to change their worlds" are "quite aware of what they're going through," and he commanded the old guard step aside for their youthful betters. These "children" were, Bowie sang elsewhere on *Hunky Dory*, "the start of a coming race." But only one year later, in "All the Young Dudes," the youth revolution had already stalled out:

And my brothers back at home with his Beatles
      and his Stones
We never got it off on that revolution stuff
What a drag, too many snags.

This completely abandons *Hunky Dory*'s visions of an American-style ascendant global youth culture. What's more, it's telling that Bowie shrugs off the breakup of "that revolution stuff" with such flippancy — he might have been lamenting a hole in a sweater or sock. In one year, then, the ambition and hope of a global utopianism has been reduced to a subcultural celebration of the minor pleasures to be found flouting the conventions of a strictly national, English, culture. In "All the Young Dudes," Bowie contracts the frame of reference, scaling back what counts as meaningful political and social action. The song invests its jouissance in distinctions of taste and minor deviation from national cultural norms. Bowie finds pleasure in demotic Cockney slang ("funky little boat race [funny face]"), minor deviations in sensibility (the championing of T. Rex over Beatles and Rolling Stones), and the small thrills of petty crime (shoplifting from Marks and Spencer). In another particularizing, localizing gesture, he name-checks his real-life London friends Freddie Burretti and Wendy Kirby.

Here was one of the many moments in Bowie's career when a hardwired faddishness allowed sociological foresight into the near future. Through *aesthetic* premonition that the Stones were passé (before *Exile!*), Bowie receives a glimpse of the *political* shortcomings of the New Left. In short, Bowie was so attuned to transformations in style, he often got a preview of coming changes in the economic and political base.

Already in 1971, Bowie was proclaiming "Rule Britannia is out of bounds." But this feeling was limited to the kooks of Haddon Hall. By 1974 it had become general. On *Diamond Dogs'* "We Are the Dead," the lament of English Tommies from the poem "In Flanders Field" — *we are the dead* — has shockingly become universally applicable. Bowie's "we" statements describe collective dependency, compromise, and confinement:

- We're fighting with the eyes of the blind.
- We feel that we are paper, choking on you nightly.
- We're today's scrambled creatures, locked in tomorrow's double features.
- Because of all we've seen, because of all we've said, we are the dead.

These pronouncements are delicately poised, still applicable to national subjects but now also transnational agents ("press men," "financiers") and subjects (consumers of media spectacle and its "twenty-four-hour service"). In Bowie's new global collapse anthems, the only bonds are trauma bonds, born of a shared subjection previously experienced only by particular groups (e.g., young English soldiers) but now commonly experienced as living death.

Meanwhile in 1970 America, Curtis Mayfield had already seen the future first with "(Don't Worry) If There's a Hell Below, We're All Gonna Go." In contrast to the counter-anthem, such national collapse anthems are purely negative. The utopian possibility for another, better nation is registered by its total absence. "Don't Worry" is an infernal vision: America is damned, beyond salvage. Civil society's drugged and hysterical, the well's poisoned, politics has been replaced with clout-chasing, everyone's exploited, and police, judges, and juries are shot through with the same corruption.

President Richard Nixon's mantra "Don't worry, worry, worry, worry," an anthemic utterance of the old sort, in Mayfield becomes pure gaslighting. A year later, Marvin Gaye sang of America as a land of social death: "The way they do my life / this ain't living." And three years after Gaye's *What's Going On*, Bob Dylan would be crying of an "idiot wind, blowing like a circle 'round my skull / from the Grand Coulee Dam to the Capitol," in the process turning Guthrie's New Deal anthem "Grand Coulee Dam" inside out. The old American national culture was now conceived in these inverted anthems via infernal terms. These songs — stirring, alternately melancholic or rampaging in tone, still addressing the nation in elevated tones — kept the stylistic shell of the old anthems while smashing up their affirmative ideological positions, replacing them with sign-changing travesties, bleak sociological figures, and grotesque menageries.

In the UK of the second half of the seventies, the national collapse anthem would culminate in punk manifestoes: the Sex Pistols' "God Save the Queen" and "Anarchy in the U.K."; the Clash's "Remote Control," "English Civil War," and "London Calling"; Crass's "Systematic Death"; the Ruts' "Babylon's Burning"; Discharge's "A Look at Tomorrow"; and so on. In less florid language and with more rage than hymnal meditation, these songs also inverted and negated the propaganda songs of British national unity, modernizing rather than abandoning their sound structure entirely.

As Paul Gilroy argued of the period in *"There Ain't No Black in the Union Jack,"* various genres of reggae, Rastafarian ideology — from Bob Marley to Brother D and through to early Yellowman — mocked the inward, defensive self-definitions of postcolonial Britain and their sense of the nation as a closed system that rightly belongs to "whites," not "immigrants." They favored cross-racial and cross-class appeal, with its utopian, "syncretic," and diasporic form and contents.[12]

At the same time as the above counter-anthems and national collapse anthems were germinating, another form, the *anthemic* pop song, was also being born. When Lester Bangs uses the word "anthemic" to describe English garage rockers the Troggs' "I Can't Control Myself" in 1971, he's sheepish: he calls the adjective "pretentious" and himself "brassy" for using it. This, along with his scare quotes, shows that *anthemic* was then an unfamiliar and recent coinage. It might not be the first deployment of the term in the modern sense, but it's *early*. The word and concept *anthemic* allows Bangs to wax poetically in his next paragraph about the

Troggs' "sexual anthems" and the supposedly "truly democratic attitude about fucking" in their song "Give It to Me."[13] The Troggs' singer, we are told, cares about his partner's pleasure: Bangs here sets the bar for erotic equality pretty low. His frivolous conflation of teen sex with democracy shows that the anthemic's relation to politics is more tenuous that the anthem's. This pop form sounds like an anthem but in contradistinction to, say, Gilroy's reggae, carries no message. With the term *anthemic*, Bangs is conceptualizing a minor anthem, without world-historical stakes, a political neutralization and formal hollowing of the old form's scale and scope.

This is where Queen reenters the story. The band first charted with 1974's *Queen II* but didn't break big internationally until 1975's *A Night at the Opera*. Though Queen is now best remembered for "Bohemian Rhapsody," not everyone recalls that *A Night at the Opera* ends with a compact (1 minute, 12 seconds), sprightly instrumental: "God Save the Queen." This Brian May claimed was a tribute to Hendrix's rendition of "The Star-Spangled Banner" six years prior. It also cites the expected conclusion to a British night at the opera: the orchestra playing the anthem.

It represents the anthem as entertainment, in other words, as *anthemic*: just another song, the occasional for a virtuosic guitar workout, a fun but neutralized version. Deideologized of both its traditional meaning and Hendrix's, it is an English product made for easy global export. Neither patriotic nor unpatriotic, not a turbulent counter-anthem nor antagonistic negative national anthem, it excites most as a brilliant translation of an old song into a seventies rock guitar instrumental. It's a heuristic closure device for *A Night at the Opera*, an expression of neither propaganda nor high art.

A minor anthem, which cites the national context blankly, the song burdens the listener with no ideology. It's of a piece with Brian May's Elektra Records letter jacket in the video for "Somebody to Love" and Freddie Mercury's comparison of Queen's music to Bic razors and used tissues: "They can listen to it, like it, discard it, then on to the next. Disposable pop."[14] Queen created anthems manqué. To reverse Joy Division's phrase, they have the feeling but have lost the spirit. From Jimmy Buffett's "Margaritaville" (1977) to Charli XCX's "Anthems" (2020), the anthemic form yearly grew in power, swelling toward the hegemony it possesses in the culture industry today.

By the second half of the seventies, the pop anthemic increasingly took on international shapes. The apolitical anthem, embracing its commodification as pure pop, was instrumental or used the restricted vocabulary of an internationally accessible Globish English. Here ABBA was the pioneer. They sang with recognizably Scandinavian accents but with a completely non-threatening, defanged, and endearing exoticism. Few concrete specifics of Swedish life or politics entered the music. The band ABBA was different but not threatening, and its deviations from standard English endearing, not provocative.

The counter-anthem and the national collapse anthem also took on international dimensions post-1968. The broadcast of

"All You Need Is Love" (1968), during an early televised satellite simulcast, begins with the fanfare of "La Marseillaise," turning the French national anthem into the intro for a global counteranthem. Expressing the utopian hopes of the time, the Beatles self-consciously position their own song as an international counter-anthem, cosmopolitan not national. In experimental music, the left-field electronic recombination of the world's national anthems in Karlheinz Stockhausen's *Hymnen* (*Anthems*, finalized 1969) was a more bracing manifestation of the same planetary impulse.

But John Lennon's "Imagine" (1971), inspired by *The Communist Manifesto*, puts a negative sign in front of "All You Need Is Love." It itemizes all we *don't* need for the world to live as one: "religion," "countries," or "possessions." In Lennon's trajectory alone from 1967 to 1971, from the Beatles to his early solo career, we hear a transition from an internationalist celebration of already-existing love to an abolitionist utopianism: a better international order can be figured only in dreams and the imagination. These songs are of a piece with modernist poet W. H. Auden and cellist Pablo Casals's "Hymn to the United Nations" (also 1971). In this internationalist collaboration—an "ode to world peace," as the *New York Times* called it—Auden strikes the "elated, optative" imperative: "Let music for peace be the paradigm." But at the same time, he begrudgingly acknowledges that "with words we lie, can say peace, when we mean war."

In Nigeria, Fela Kuti epics like "Water No Get Enemy" (1975) and "International Thief Thief" (1979) straddled the line between geopolitical counter-anthems and anthems of global collapse. In a just world, water would be an inalienable human right and kept unpolluted, uncommodified, and free for all: a universal resource. But "International Thief Thief" articulates the global realpolitik that keeps even elemental substances like water hoarded, degraded, and politically manipulated. In this world, direct colonial brutality has given way to informal corporate colonialism:

> *Many foreign companies dey Africa*
> *Carry all our money go*
> ....
> *They go dey cause confusion*
> *Cause corruption*
> *Cause oppression*
> *Cause inflation.*

All are achieved via elite capture: the grooming and bribing of African leaders until they serve the interests of foreign multi-nationals: "Commissioner, Permanent Secretary, Minister, Head of State."

Others in the late seventies and early eighties dodged anthemic forms entirely. Whether because it seemed politically suspect for crowds to sing in unison or because anthemic music increasingly began to feel embarrassing, genres as wide-ranging as new age and no wave, minimalism, dub and *kosmische*, ambient and free jazz tended to avoid the bombastic monumentality of anthemic music for tranquil, slowly mutating process tones or skronking horns, slowly churning bass loops, repetitions with minor variations, or atonal meanders. Even disco, as it mutated into boogie and "disco not disco," lost its grand live strings and huge choruses. In many of the cutting-edge genres and modes of the era, the pop anthem was only a present absence.

On the smaller-scale, anthems were also being written for DIY labels addressing subcultures and scenes beneath the national and transnational ones. One example is Red Krayola's single "Born in Flames" (1980) for Rough Trade Records. A mock anthem for Lizzie Borden's near-future feminist film of the same name, the song is laced with leftist slogans delivered with varying levels of seriousness. Its audience was intentionally limited to a fraction of a fraction: absurdist weirdos with a penchant for critical theory.

American hardcore bands like Bad Brains, Minor Threat, Black Flag, and Dead Kennedys initially had no interest in mass pop crossover. Anthems like "Straight Edge," "Banned in D.C.," "Nervous Breakdown," and "California Über Alles" sought audiences in local DIY niches, youth subcultures, and class fractions, while actively antagonizing those outside of them. Of course, these niche anthems became more broadly popular only after their historical moment had passed.

In all the subgenres of funk, soul, and boogie, newly modified by adjectives like *outsider*, *personal*, *private*, *lo-fi*, and *basement* and now avidly sought by music collectors, micro-anthems were proliferating. These were records pressed locally just once and in small runs. On tape, home-recording pioneer R. Stevie Moore had begun *Bedroom Radio* on WFMU and was just about to launch his Cassette Club; underground tape-trading in the burgeoning thrash, speed, and black metal scenes was bubbling up to the surface. These networks of listeners and musicians were bound together by anthems never meant for prime time.

The same musical minorness could be found anywhere on the globe. These included a variety of different interventions in non-rock and rock-adjacent genres, from factional roots reggae (Rex Harley's ode to Grenadian insurgents in the Marxist New Jewel Movement, "Dread in a PRA" [1979]) to the alternative-lifestyle shadow plays of goth kicked off by Bauhaus's "Bela Lugosi's Dead" (1979), Horace Tapscott and the Pan Afrikan Peoples Arkestra's minimal spiritual jazz-piano-and-small-chorus take on "Lift Every Voice and Sing" (1979, the "Black national anthem"), or Serge Gainsbourg's divisive cod reggae twist on "La Marseillaise," "Aux Armes et cætera" (1979). These and other experiments were anti-universalist anthems, intended not for easy, universal co-optation but for some tinier vanguard subculture, minor either in taste, political experience, or communal affiliation.

In this wave, when a known anthem like William Blake's "Jerusalem" was covered, it was to completely rewrite its meaning. Like Gainsbourg's "Aux Armes," Mark Stewart (post–Pop Group) turned to reggae, specifically dub, for a 1982 cover to crack wide open the sort of traditional nationalist version you might hear after the BBC Proms. Meanwhile, in Christchurch, New Zealand, in 1981, Flying Nun Records released the Clean's "Tally Ho!," a strong contender for the first "indie rock" anthem. By 1981, more and more DIY anthems were being produced for niche, sometimes subhistorical audiences. Anthems were no longer just for divinities, nations, and international mass movements.

This was the field of historical forces ca. 1981 — political, aesthetic, and social — out of which Queen and David Bowie's pop anthem "Under Pressure" emerged. New pop anthems were spinning out in multiple, often contradictory modes, united only by the shared sense that new experiments in this social form were necessary. Necessary because the old collective bonds were broken, and the old forms that had helped secure and produce them (for better *and* worse) no longer had the power to do either.

But what's this have to do with "Under Pressure"? Well, despite the inherent imprecision of such specific dating, it might be said that 1981, the year the song was released, was year zero for our own contemporary historical moment. As Fredric Jameson recently re-periodized the 1980s in 2016, "It seems to me that everybody recognizes some kind of postmodern break, whatever name they give it, *that takes place around 1980 or so*, in the Reagan/Thatcher era, with the advent of economic deregulation, the new salience of globalization."[15] The world of this "postmodern break," dawning then, has been wholly subsumed as second nature today. And in the realm of pop, by 1984, the corporate recording industry had already locked music down, consolidating what Michaelangelo Matos has felicitously termed "the golden age of corporate synergy."[16] Not coincidentally, 1981 was the year the pop anthem started congealing into its two regnant forms: rousing anthems of the private writ large (e.g., "'Heroes'") and world-encompassing anthemic entertainment without any content whatsoever (e.g., "We Will Rock You"/"We Are the Champions").

So, by returning to "Under Pressure," we return to a pop anthem from the moment of our present moment's emergence. "Under Pressure" offers us concepts, diagnoses, and structures of feeling from a moment when the destruction of our collective lives and the corruption of our institutions (primarily but not limited to state and corporation) were in the offing but not yet felt and assumed to be irresistible, inevitable, and irreversible. "Under Pressure" represents the collision of Bowie's and Queen's opposed experiments with collective being.

"Under Pressure," like all great pop anthems, attempts to process the contradictions and conflicts built into communal life. No matter how much we try to retreat or subtract ourselves from the necessity of collective existence, we need others. Pop music's contribution is to model and inculcate in us the rudiments of future social glues.

In other words, anthems work by "providing reference points for an experiment which exceeds our capacities to foresee."[17]

But such "experiments" in pop are as much practical as utopian: songs like "Under Pressure" renew the search for useful forms of sociality.

It should go without saying that I'm not claiming that we are only *x* number of pop anthems away from staving off the apocalypse. Rather, the point is that without the affective affirmation and imaginative negation produced and provided by works like "Under Pressure," it will be much more difficult to imagine that structural change is possible. When it comes to popular aesthetic forms, none articulates the problems, symptoms, and scales of collective breakdown, or generates more experiments (in thought and feeling) toward remedying that breakdown, than the pop anthem.

But what made "Under Pressure" a work that so powerfully represented its era that it still has things to teach us today? Going into the recording of "Under Pressure," Bowie and Queen represented two conflicting versions of this pop anthem ("'Heroes'" vs. "We Will Rock You"). In combative collaboration, they needed to produce a third style: "Under Pressure" is both a combination of and a sound outside Bowie's and Queen's other productions. Working together required the invention of new ways of working, recording, writing, and performing. But it was also because both Bowie and Queen were savvy students of the history of pop music genres, of the behavior and tastes of crowds and mass life. This added a second-order, conceptual dimension to the song.

The strange, dense, hybrid character of "Under Pressure" is also a historical phenomenon — it can be considered the culmination of fatigue with more immediate forms of pop anthem.

This context spurred Queen and Bowie to build a layer of self-critique into their anthem. Finally, the unique genesis of the song, recorded spur-of-the-moment in Switzerland and remixed a week later in NYC, meant that the released version would of course be a second-order interpretation of its impromptu Swiss raw materials. Not only was there a week's gap for the artists to reflect on what they would do with the initial tracks, but in the mixdown, a whole new anthem stepped into view.

What's more, Bowie's and Mercury's peculiarities as artists blended and clashed throughout the development of the song. For example, Bowie's penchant for avant abstraction interrupts Mercury's love of melodramatic excess, while the two had a shared obsession with glam camp rhyme. It was this dynamic, fraught, and contradictory collaboration that gave the song a complexity and enduring frisson that still powerfully sounds today.

But because "Under Pressure" is a composite work — critics have described its "cut-and-paste feel" — it juxtaposes and inter-relates competing modes of the pop anthem, without being reducible to any one.[18] Like most of the anthems cataloged above, it is rousing and catchy and articulates a collective struggle on a grand narrative scale. But as we will see, it is neither a national anthem, a counter-national anthem, a niche anthem, an evacuated pastiche, a straightforward hymn, nor a fight song. And due to its ambiguous, multifarious status, its volatile vortexing of all of its genre's touchstones, even the best critics, like Ned Raggett, have settled for dubbing it "anthemic" and calling it a day.[19]

Philosopher Simon Critchley's *Bowie* doesn't mention it, and Shelton Waldrep's academic study *Future Nostalgia: Performing David Bowie* references it only once; Chris O'Leary's *Ashes to Ashes* deems it powerful but suspect, a "sad hippie song beneath its cannonades and arias," trumped up by its two singers' enthusiasm "into being far better than it deserves to be."[20] It's not featured in the recent Bowie documentary *Moonage Daydream* or the Queen biopic *Bohemian Rhapsody*. Hardcore Queen fans are more appreciative of the song's merits than Bowie's. Even Bowie himself got into the judgmental spirit years after the song's recording, claiming to be embarrassed by some of the song's lyrics, and said the track "stands up best as a demo."[21]

Yet despite this touchy avoidance (cut with condescension) by critics, the song is well known and well loved by non-critics and casual fans. It's a karaoke and radio staple, Vanilla Ice took its bassline from famous to super-famous in 1990, and boilerplate-brained Bill Gates recently named it a desert island disc (gauchely and anachronistically associating it with "disco days with a bit of weekend fun"[22]). In *Happy Feet Two*, a children's movie so dire its writer said he'd rather be shot in the head than write a third installment, corporate cartoon penguins and walruses cloyingly duet "Under Pressure," and it themes an incredibly irritating

Minions trailer. So it's the sort of song CEOs namedrop to playact as men of the people and movie studios cravenly insert into cash grabs. It's been loved to the point of overfamiliarity.

Like all great pop, "Under Pressure" is easy to enjoy and difficult to interpret. Many critics have perhaps tamped down their enthusiasm of "Under Pressure" to avoid being thought middlebrow. While triangulating the song's cultural capital is fun, it does not begin to interpret the song. It's more interesting to think about the song as a zone where mass enjoyment and critical interpretation meet and misrecognize one another.

Any complete reading of "Under Pressure" must account for the contradictory space where popular fandom's breezy assessments meet more elaborated readings of the song's historical context and aesthetic form. So this book will treat "Under Pressure" as a nexus of contesting interpretations and uses — the site where popular and critical discourse touch, converse, and contradict one another. As we'll see, this sort of fraught relation is already built into the form of the song itself, in the "duet" and "duel" of Bowie and Mercury's performances and in the two visions for the song smashed together into the song's "compromise" issued version.[23]

To untangle the significances of "Under Pressure," I've chosen to follow what we might call the song's three primary keywords, in the order they appear — *pressure*, *streets*, and *love* — devoting a chapter to each. As these terms are enmeshed and interwoven in the song, it may seem procrustean and too literal-minded to parse them this way. But as "Under Pressure" is a song that accumulates power and meaning as its duet form develops, following its unfolding from beginning to middle to end is essential.

And to do so, we first have to clear the detritus of the song's contemporary meaning — the result of so many corporate captures, dilutions, travesties, and cynical citations — the now automatic and accepted manipulations of the musical past by today's culture industry. Any pop music critic's first role is to recontextualize, reinterpret, rehistoricize, and so redeem a past work and lift it out of its weakened state as dead metaphor.

If a song like "Under Pressure" is to again have meaning for us today, a double action must be performed. First, its roots in and relations to its own historical moment must be redescribed. For its aesthetic and affective potential to be reactivated for contemporary listeners, it needs to be reheard in such a way that burns away the ice of long misuse and unhearing. Once this is done, the song's historically situated meaning can be put back in touch with the crises and concerns of our present.

In doing so, we'll trace the intertwined relation between the modern pop anthem, collective politics, and the dominant institutions of state, corporation, and civil society in the past forty years. It's my belief that a close reading of "Under Pressure" will reveal the pop anthem to be a pivotal clearinghouse for the collective imagination.

The pop anthem, as the most ambitious and affecting producer of collective sentiment, and the only pop genre that pretends to conceptualize society in toto, is both a bellwether for the state of collective politics and a means for thinking and feeling beyond its present limits. And as no song both critiqued and embodied the contradictions and techniques of its genre more thoroughly, all theories of the popular anthem must go through Bowie and Queen's "Under Pressure."

▶ 01 Pressure

TO BEGIN WITH AN ETYMOLOGICAL GAME: The word *pressure* shares Latin roots with expression/impression/depression/oppression/repression. *Pressure* is derived from *pressura*, which indicates pressing, squeezing, crushing, a throng, and a burden. Taken most literally, *expression* means a squeezing out, like juice from grapes, and *impression*, the use of pressure to "imprint or stamp" on or into something.[1] They all share an even earlier Proto-Indo-European root in *per-*, which means "to strike."

This shared nexus of meaning uncovers a mnemotechnics, the production of memory by force, still operative today. In contemporary life, pressure is the concept for the transformation of actual violence into ambient violence, what Bowie called in 1977 "slaughter in the air." Pressure occurs where the literal pain of being struck and crushed becomes internalized as a burden, where the world's expressions are subjectively impressed into us. If given only two words to encapsulate the connection between aesthetics and politics, art and real life, we could do much worse than saying that contemporary life produces aesthetics *under pressure*.

But this is a broad proposition. Historically, there were specifically so many pressure songs in the seventies and early eighties because pressure is the concept and feel of economic, social, and political deadlock. Pressure builds when the stress and violence of life lived inside contradictions is not allowed release. When people need things they cannot have, there is pressure. When collective projects that protect and advance genuine liberty, equality, and solidarity are foreclosed, there is pressure. And when all lines of flight seem blocked: pressure.

Pressure proliferates in moments when the dialectic stalls out — when thesis and antithesis continually collide without transcendence into a revolutionary synthesis. "Get up offa that thang and try to release that pressure!" James Brown exhorted, but he knew that even the temporary release of dancing wasn't promised by 1976. On "Hell" two years earlier, he'd sung:

> *Say Brother, tell them, it's hell*
> *If you're Jewish it's hell*
> *If you're Black it's hell*
> *If you're White it's hell, poor white*
> *If you're, uh, if you're Indian, it's hell.*

Under pressure, boredom and terror infernally circulate and combine.

As a pop music conceit, pressure was apposite because it was broadly applicable. It was neither a slangy shibboleth of the sort

Bowie sometimes favored in the seventies ("peopleoids," "blam-blam," "Kether to Malkhuth") nor one of the shopworn phrases Queen used in even their best songs ("losing my beat," "you're my sunshine," "I'm a shooting star").

In "Pressure Drop," Toots and the Maytals' reggae classic, pressure is karma, which Toots wishes upon a discrete foe.[2] And with a studied, nostalgic look backward to Toots's era, two-tone ska revivalists the Selecter's "Too Much Pressure" (1980) also treats pressure as optional for some "certain kind of people / them having it easy." Pressure, in the older and older-minded songs, was still optional, something suffered by certain individuals, classes, or races but not others.

But by the era of "Under Pressure," pressure had become ubiquitous, diffuse but dreadfully powerful. In the songs of the era, pressure appears as an autochthonous force of universal stress. It collapses boundaries between internal and external, local and global, micro and macro — pressure is the malevolent spirit of one world under pressure.

On Earl Zero's roots classic "Only Jah" (1979), the only solution to this omnipotent force is otherworldly: "Only Jah can ease the pressure." On the Units' synth-punk masterpiece "High Pressure Days" (1979), under pressure the narrator and his friends resemble "slippery kelp," "hot H_2O molecules," and "bumping cars." They're pinballing subjects to a pressure impossible to resist, which dictates the pace, direction, and shape of social relations.

Even notoriously antisocial Ray Davies worries his pressure could become social contagion on the throwaway Kinks track "Pressure" (1979); James Blood Ulmer and Negative Approach's tracks of the same name, in free jazz (1980) and hardcore (1982) respectively, manifest pressure's power in form.

Pressure in this moment was a figure for frustration: history had stopped progressing. Pressure represents either an unavoidable block to desire, escapable only in dreams of magic, the divine, or utopia. Pressure is the name for things that won't change, that used to be amenable to transformation by individuals, collectives, or institutions.

A pop anthem stands between the audience and the larger institution it represents. It is there to motivate people to identify with, believe in, follow, and advance a group ideal into the future via individual and collective action. But pressure, insofar as it is antidialectic, a force that produces motion but not progress, seemed by its very nature anti-anthemic. Pressure in its real-world manifestations — failed revolutions, the rise of revanchism, CIA sabotage, neoliberal atomization — all froze belief in individual, institutional, and collective will. In the dominant usage of the time in pop, from reggae to synth punk, pressure is the name for all the things in the real world that delegitimize the traditional base for the anthem.

In this context, "Under Pressure" represents a new form. Its differences register and respond to the new historical context. First, unlike most anthems, "Under Pressure" is a duet-and-duel between dissimilar vocalists. Traditional anthems, of course, depend on a call-and-response between a soloist or choir and a crowd — the word *anthem*, after all, comes from the Greek *antiphona* for "verse response." Bowie and Mercury sing in dialogue, and occasionally in unison, but just as frequently in combat and a spirit of contradiction.

The format militates against feelings of unity. Its dynamic, unsettled version of the pop anthem is alien to past anthems' push to consolidate a fused front. But these were different times.

The presentation and representation of pressure begins with the collision between two very different singers, Bowie and Mercury, and between different styles of pop. The tension between the two artists results not from their absolute opposition — they were English, at various times performed glam rock, wrote anthems, were relatively rather than alienatingly strange, and sailed the same troubled waters between the broad mainstream and the narrow minor experiment. Bowie and Mercury were both what now could be called queer, international celebrities, and in 1981 each was just beginning to descend from his commercial and critical zenith. This is what gives the song its mixed, ambiguously shifting, and multileveled sound, feel, and meaning — Bowie and Queen share enough concepts, styles, lifestyles, and images to compete over the same musical raw materials.

In this, they allegorize 1981's world of pressure — a world in which shared proximity to the same global cultures, problems, and ways of thinking and creating no longer sustain stark oppositions but will not produce group fusions or even solidaristic alliances. In a world in which melodramatic, world-historical overcomings occurred, the total victory of a single class, nation, religion, or way of life seemed impossible. What was left even in pop music? Endless competition to put a new spin on the same old forms.

But because anthems cannot entirely do away with the framework of villains and heroes, challenge and its overcoming, in "Under Pressure" we encounter a different sort of enemy, a concretized abstraction. Pressure has gained the ability to kill and maim. Bowie and Mercury's concept of "pressure," ca. 1981, can join the ranks of so many other mostly invisible but palpable abstract forces in society — debt, credit, authority, guilt, damnation, salvation, and all the other human inventions that have taken on lives of their own.

Unwittingly, Bowie and Queen had independently been preparing to analyze, allegorize, and embody the pressure of the times. First, both were experts in multitracking vocals. The master tape for "Bohemian Rhapsody" had so many vocal lines bounced and overdubbed onto it that one can now see through it. The band's studio prowess meant their vocals, using just three voices, could sound massive in unison and range high and low on their own — you can hear the whole bag of tricks on "Somebody to Love." More subtle was Mercury's double-tracking, which allowed two noticeably different line-readings to run in parallel.

Similarly, Bowie sang with himself in the studio with more verve than any other musician since the invention of recorded music. He broke through with "Space Oddity." This was originally a duet, with John Hutchinson playing the role of Ground Control and Bowie, Major Tom. The version we know, however, features Bowie playing both characters, as well as intoning the lift-off countdown. What's more, in it a matter-of-fact lower voice is panned completely to the left, while a higher, nervier one takes up the entire right channel. The subliminal effect is to enact cognitive dissonance between the safety of earth and the void of space, and so captures Major Tom's impossible feelings — of outward speed and inner stillness, of seeing the whole earth from millions of miles away.

Bowie's novelty track "The Laughing Gnome" uses sped-up vocals for the part of the gnome. And his cover of Pink Floyd's "See Emily Play" employs a distorted second voice on the chorus to inject Syd Barrett's contemporaneous mental breakdown under the surface of an otherwise faithful rendition. On "Candidate," Bowie's multitracking projects a multiplied power into the voice of a sinister politician. And he fittingly provides all the voices for the celestial choir in his Christian-but-self-regarding "Word on a Wing."

For the song "Scream Like a Baby," a sped-up, deepened voice represents the duress of subjection to behaviorist mind control by a neofascist regime (the man was simply too into *1984*). Bowie's voice was always versatile: even when he was not manipulating and layering in post-production, a single performance might veer from style to style, from low baritone to spoken word to falsetto. While Queen used multitracked vocals for effects of monumental choruses and Mercury's bravura leads, Bowie tended to use them for moments of splitting: the breaking apart of unitary perspective and the undermining of earnest grand statements.

So both Bowie and Queen went into the studio together with a great deal of experience recording, producing, and combining human singing voices. Maybe too much: strong opinions made for a fractious mixdown session at New York's Power Station a week after roughs were recorded in Switzerland's Mountain Studios. After a marathon twenty-four-hour session, Bowie, Mercury, Roger Taylor, and producer Reinhold Mack settled on a compromise mix no one alone would have chosen (May notes, "Someone has to back off").[3]

The tension resulted in the production of a third sound unlike either party. The song is a grouping of attacks, of musical styles and points of view — it is a set of anti-pressure tactics, often opposed or even contradictory, rather than the presentation of one overarching strategy. The Queen polish is missing and gone are the walls of stacked vocals; Bowie does no experiments with vocal personas and no subliminal self-accompaniment.

On the other hand, the song is anything but a no-frills duet. Inspired by his and Brian Eno's Berlin experiments with aleatoric technique, Bowie convinced Mercury they should each record their vocals separately, without hearing what the other was singing. This way, they might create something spontaneous and fresh, unconditioned by foreknowledge. But even this Rawlsian scheme to establish a veil of ignorance between collabora-tors turned into another source of pressure: Bowie cheated, lis-tening in on Mercury's takes and tailoring his own in response. This results in a dualistic relation that runs throughout the per-formance, in which Mercury's parts are more spontaneous and naive than Bowie's, which are critical responses. This is not a song in which the enemy of pressure can be overcome once and for all through peaceful collaboration. Brian May remembers a "fierce battle."[4]

Antagonism is the general framework out of which momentary glimpses of togetherness, union, and solidarity come together. But they are momentary and not the culmination or canceling of pressure. In fact, power asymmetries persisted throughout the recording process. In these struggles Bowie's vision tended to prevail: he deleted May's cringeworthy (both lyrically and aurally) vocal verse about the powerful and powerless, rewrote the words around the central concept "under pressure," and even touched John Deacon's bass while he was playing the signature riff to correct him and dominated the mixdown in New York. When May enthused during the original jam that the song "sounded like The Who!," Bowie rejoined, "It won't when we're done with it!"[5]

In more than half its moments, "Under Pressure" is much more Bowie-with-Queen than the reverse. He suggested they work up an original rather than continue with Cream covers, he decided how the vocals would be recorded, and he "fixed" the bassline.

As a result, it's easy to think of the relation between Bowie's and Mercury's voices as a simple opposition. This is how duets that take the form of a back-and-forth dialogue — whether June Carter Cash and Johnny Cash's G-rated "Jackson" or Notorious B.I.G. and Lil' Kim's X-rated "Another" — tend to take shape. June and Lil' Kim take one side of a clear argument, Johnny and Biggie the other, and they fight it out. This style leaves open the possibility of rapprochement, of a resolution. The playful tone signals that these aren't irrevocable breaks but rather differences of position that might be solved through a private understanding.

If forced to read "Under Pressure" as such a duet, we could boil down the seeming differences between the two like this:

INITIAL PERSONA OPPOSITIONS IN "UNDER PRESSURE"

Mercury	Bowie
Open	Guarded
Impressionist	Expressionist
Lyrical/Romantic	Gloomy/Gothic
Transcendence-seeking	Immanence-exploring
Apolitical	Committed

But "Under Pressure" doesn't work this way. As a song born of and obsessed with pressure erasing the boundary between outside and inside, impression and expression, it dispenses with the stability of expected character types. When the enemy is not an amorous rival or the errancy of a loved one but an internalized historical force like pressure, the solution cannot be a revised contract between two loved ones.

Bowie and Mercury are not struggling in a game with winners and losers, a wrong answer and a correct one: the song has no interest in proving which side of any of the dualisms above should prevail. Rather, they are testing new connections and combinations between these positions. The song is a series of experiments to make poles crisscross, run in parallel, and clash in productive ways. A look at the shifting inflections of the figure pressure itself will help us unpack matters.

Sonically, the first appearance of pressure in the song is explosive. In the video, Bowie's urgent, commanding, and expanding first *"Pressure!"* is paired with footage of a piece of machinery detonating into a fireball. This big bang gives the feeling of pressure spreading out, penetrating previously unreached spaces, and saturating all around it. On first listen, nothing prepares for this sudden eruption. What precedes it is the song's rhythmic baseline: hand claps and snaps, plinking two-chord piano riff, and infamous bassline.

This insistent looping of rhythms defines the default level of tension in "Under Pressure," a constant, infectious, slightly off-kilter pattern designed to lock in the listener's attention. It is a reined-in, regular loop — and perhaps because the song was a remix of the initial recording session, from the beginning it sounded and functioned like a hip-hop sample (ten years before Vanilla Ice decided to rap a Black fraternity chant over it).

Brian May's chiming twelve-string gently joins the mix, and then begins Mercury's scatted, improvised vocables. These are plaintive and lyrical, the sound of someone singing by themselves but hoping to be overheard. Then Bowie's "*PRESSure!*" comes stepping in and blows the setup to smithereens. His is the sound of a force that pushes and presses on the great and the small, on inanimate and animate alike. In Bowie's inaugural line-read of the word, the brakes come off and the song accelerates — there's no way back to the tenderness and manageable tension of Queen's introduction. On Bowie's entry, Roger Taylor's drums kick in with a pounding sense of rising tension. The vocals from this point further ratchet up the stress.

After Bowie announces the theme, it's as if Mercury has been snapped out of a reverie. Bowie then sings "under pressure" again with the same gloomy force of its first announcement, but this time Mercury joins him underneath with his own line-read, in a mournful, higher tone, ascending to meet the challenge of Bowie's lower register. This transitions the vocal back to Mercury alone, who quickly narrates that pressure is breaking up families and burning down homes, only to quickly hand it back to Bowie to add that it also "puts people on streets."

Mercury's undertone is airier and more empathetic than Bowie's gloomy, external view. Already, each vocal performance destabilizes the last. The song is a series of cascading responses, requests not to meet in the middle but for each vocalist to follow the other, to deal with a higher stage of sonic and affective pressure. Mercury's reading of the line "under pressure" incorporates the heightened anxiety of Bowie's, mixing it with his initial, more meditative one. Pressure rises, and the system becomes more dynamic as a result.

This is duet not as dialogue toward compromise and shared understanding but as a dynamic process in which two voices come together to produce a third perspective that exceeds the limits of their individual positions. In other words, it's a dialectic, not a dualism. This process continues in the third instance of pressure in the song, Bowie's "pressure on people / people on streets." This rejoins Mercury's most hopeful lyric up to this point in the song: "Tomorrow, get me higher." Bowie's tone is, in turn, leavened by Mercury's outlandish gambit at transcendence, while insisting on the force of pressure pushing down on Mercury's fancy.

From this point in the song, Bowie alone sings the "pressure" and "under pressure" phrases. After Mercury's verse about kicking his "brains round the floor," the song returns to another round of Mercury vocables and Bowie's bridge about terror. It is repetition with a difference, this return to "terror" and "pressure on people" building in the listener a further desire for the next breakthrough from Mercury's side.

This comes after Mercury and Queen feint a slowdown, the verse about the dangers of quietism, in which Mercury says he once "turned away from it all like a blind man." A gospel-organ-sounding KORG hums in the background, and Mercury briefly falls into the realm of sacred song, the ur-form of the anthem. Think of Little Richard's on "Tutti Frutti": "I don't mean that it's a hymn — like an anthem in church — but it's nothing bad about it. A song of love and joy in a world of chaos and commotion and strife."[6] But even this moment of the most reflective tranquility must be shattered. Mercury is singing of the impossibility of becoming a Hegelian beautiful soul and of the need for engagement: "It don't work," he concludes. This is a false pause, a rest you know will be abandoned.

This gives way to one of the song's most hair-raisingly sublime moments: Bowie's vicious interruption of Mercury's idyll with "INSANITY LAUGHS, UNDER PRESSURE WE'RE CRACKING." Here Bowie takes on the voice of insanity, his most goth moment in the era of Bauhaus and Siouxsie Sioux. Chris O'Leary has dismissed the "brutal syntax" of this line, but its broken word order mirrors the disorder of madness, both in individual and collective effect. If Bowie had delivered the line in the King's English (e.g., "Insanity laughs and we're cracking under pressure"), it would have had too logical a feel and undermined the grandeur and stakes of the song's development up to this crisis point.

Bowie sketches a problem (pressure), Mercury presents a potential solution ("tomorrow" and the possibility of the future), Bowie negates and unravels that solution (terror has already staked a claim on the future), and Mercury returns with a new solution that anticipates Bowie's past critique (commitment to the here and now is a more specific form of praxis), only for Bowie's most forceful vision of the odds against progressive action (general insanity mocks the hope for such change, and the ubiquitous force of pressure has begun cracking us all).

The movement of the song is toward an attempted musical (symbolic) resolution of the recondite, unremovable pressure of the real world. In its relentless push toward higher and higher levels of duet, the song elaborates an attempted struggle out of deadlock. Restless, the song stages collision after collision between hopeful and practical forms of action to test their limits and hopefully produce a version that can withstand the pressure and endure. It is a dialectical method applied to a world in which dialectics toward a better world have been halted, and people seem powerless to change state and economic processes beyond the reach of individual and popular action alike. The song's insistence on constant motion, development, and transformation from one stage to another is one reason why May's verse from the demo was left on the cutting-room floor: it ground down the propulsive motion of the song to a halt.

The form the duet takes — combative, mutually interrogative, with occasional moments of shared feeling — scandalously pushes toward a breakthrough inside a song from a time in which none seemed available outside it. Thus the song takes the form of anthem: It is mantled in heroics, a need to fight against great historical odds. Its scope is grand, and it presumes to represent the entire world in broad aesthetic strokes. But its enemy is a new sort, not a rival nation but an oppressive power that is seemingly global, ubiquitous, and yet hard to define — of the sort Michel Foucault talked about as the micropolitics found in the small rituals and practices of government and self-government he calls governmentality, as well as Deleuze's mechanisms of control: "self-deforming," adaptable forms of power, which can attach themselves to the smallest, most quotidian ways of being, thinking, and feeling.[7]

So while it's true "pressure" is a broad, diffuse target for an anthem, this should not be mistaken for a conceptual and formal defect. For example, O'Leary critiques the "vagaries" of the song's lyrics and situates "Under Pressure" in that tiresome train of "rock star 'social commentaries' [in which] the star, isolated by money and sycophants, speaks in generalities, as though fearful of alienating constituencies with an inappropriate detail."[8] But this forgets two considerations. First, the anthem necessarily speaks in generalities and has since its origins in the consolidation of religious community and nation building. It may be inspired by a particular event or individual, but it must transform these into something more abstract to appeal to a mass audience. The transformation of the already stylized "John Brown's Body" into "The Battle Hymn of the Republic" is exemplary. Just as few would remember *The Communist Manifesto* (the manifesto being the anthem's analogue in prose) if it were filled only with local interventions (e.g., its digression on nineteenth-century

Polish politics), an "Under Pressure" laden with concrete, naturalistic detail would leave it an uninteresting lump of information. The anthem necessarily must swerve away from the simple chronicle and catalog to do what it does and reach who it reaches.

Second, to return to the historical situation of the early eighties: in times of the defeat of emancipatory projects, strategies need to be rethought and new operations need to be performed. This goes as much for the pop song, if it is to mean something, as it does for critical theory. "Under Pressure" is a song about times dominated by a new dispensation of power and the fracturing of many of the old bonds that kept solidarity and collective projects together. In the "counter-revolution of the 1980s," even the usually stalwart militant Maoist Alain Badiou found himself "extraordinarily" affected by "the violence of the restoration ... the counter-revolutionary, ideological, theoretical restoration."[9] Given the tenor of the times, the swing of "Under Pressure" at the biggest problems of the era should not be misrecognized as the specious loftiness of out-of-touch cosmopolitan elites but seen as an attempt to reinvent minimal collective problems and language when none were objectively available in society at large.

In any case, pressure is close to but not a general concept, a suitable vehicle only for bromides and sententia, as we find in Queen's most uninspired solo moments. But pressure is a capacious conceit: this accessible language of the pop anthemic, as with the institutional anthems of old, requires such broadness. The central image of an anthem should be the midpoint between the familiar and the alien: "the star-spangled banner" is an elevated phrase for an everyday flag. "Under pressure" and "pressure" are appealing and not quite clichés, but not so wholly novel or strange to be off-putting either.

An anthem must draw its lines sharply — between friends and enemies, hopes and fears — in strokes clear enough to be intelligible and yet also to be a spur to passion and potential action in listeners. "Under Pressure" does this by connecting pressure to manifold levels of experience — subjective, objective, interpersonal, global. And the keywords of the song (pressure, people, streets, terror, love) seem to me central sites of contradiction for both 1981 and today.

What's more, many of Bowie's greatest songs preceding "Under Pressure" used allegorical figures and anthropomorphized abstractions. From this view, "Under Pressure" does not break with the older, more avant-garde Bowie, and anticipates the sellout of *Let's Dance* (1983), so much as it redirects one of its main currents. Perhaps fitting with his lifelong interest in SF, these songs tend to borrow fundamental concepts from simple physics and basic ontology — "Space Oddity" (1969), "Changes" (1971), "Time" (1973), "Shapes of Things" (Yardbirds cover, 1973), "Speed of Life" and "Sound and Vision" (both 1977), and so on. In "Ashes to Ashes" (1980), perhaps inspired by a recent viewing of Ridley Scott's *Alien* (tagline "in space no one can hear you scream"), Major Tom relates that "the shrieking of nothing is killing," giving agency and voice to the inanimate, infinite, and abstract.

In all these songs, abstractions seem more powerful and vicious than the characters: Major Tom nods out victimized by space, the narrator of "Shapes of Things" inertly wonders about the future as pretty patterns flit in front of his eyes, Time's "script is you and me" and "demands Billy Dolls and other friends of mine," and time exerts the same power in "Changes." "Speed of Life" is an instrumental but carries the listener in motion just faster than the pace of the standard walking gait. Human agency recedes, and abstract forces come alive with autochthonous power.

By contrast, in Queen, an earthy literalism and a tendency toward cliché reign. Their exuberance comes from the music and stage show, not the words. There are exceptions — the baroque coming-out allegory of "Bohemian Rhapsody," so encrypted behind commedia del arte references and flashy changes, and "Death on Two Legs (Dedicated to . . .)," in which an allegorical title turns out to be a chanson à clef about Queen's first manager.

When Queen turns to allegory, they usually mine close-to-home content from the band's history and their record labels, managers, and fans. To oversimplify, Bowie tended to write in metaphysical forms where archetypal forces dominate individuals and crowds, while Queen tended to represent their own individual history within the institutions of major-label stardom. In "Under Pressure," these two forms meet.

Mercury's monomaniacal desire for personal transcendence crashes into Bowie's skepticism about the power and reach of human agency; Mercury's operatic flights are brought to ground by Bowie's dour baritone. Mercury's inwardness and Bowie's obsession with observing externals refuse to fuse into a shared vision, and so the pressure keeps building.

Pressure in "Under Pressure," then, is a concept for life in a society in which every relationship generates friction, misunderstanding, and contradiction. Unlike the pressure in the "pressure valve theory" often (and reductively) attributed to theorist Mikhail Bakhtin by functional sociology, there's no sense within the aesthetic system of the song that a normal status quo can be returned to by rechanneling and releasing the tension elsewhere — it supersaturates every level of experience, every verse of the song. A breakthrough in one zone of pressure leads to a buildup in another. Considering the dynamic interaction between Bowie's and Mercury's voices, the song can be viewed as a series of failed attempts to release pressure.

We feel under pressure when history no longer is progressing and when attempts to produce new projects with others, whether to push toward aesthetic or political breakthroughs, often result in one experience of violent contradiction, isolation, and failure. Pressure occurs when the levels of everyday being — political, personal, aesthetic, romantic — will not unite, bond, and interweave us with one another. Bowie and Mercury model such relations in their duet, and its many thrills for the listener come in its staging of the moments of conflict, non-bonding, and fleeting feelings of escape at the heart of contemporary life. Pressure and the violent contradictions of life are constant but dynamic problems, ones that must constantly be struggled against, endured, and mitigated, without hope for final victory or despair over inevitable loss.

So pressure in "Under Pressure" takes the traditional place of the enemy in the old anthems: sin in church hymns, the rich in "The Internationale," fascist scum in "The Sacred War," old Virginia in "John Brown's Body," the dark past in "Lift Every Voice and Sing," the foreign stroke in "Rule, Britannia," and so on. But unlike in these anthems, pressure seems too built into the contemporary world for Bowie and Mercury to offer up a simple solution. When their voices join and reinforce one another, it is a transitory overlap — the song gives no sense that pressure can be permanently eradicated with some enchanted religious, political, or ethical wave of the wand. Such are the anthems, neither hopeless nor utopian, that are produced when the times are antagonistic to collective progress.

▶ 02 People

WHO IS THE SUBJECT of "Under Pressure"? This simple question can be answered simply: *people*. Not *the* people or even "people on the street," but *people*. But to understand what people means in the song, we must work through the method in which Queen and Bowie construct shared concepts and sentiments in their particular usages. One way into this is through a careful analysis of the shifting pronouns in the song, through which the collective concepts of "Under Pressure" are variously constituted and unmade throughout the song's duration. But first a short word on "Under Pressure's" anthemic time experiments with first-person plurals, its use of *we*, *us*, and *our*. This we do to map the terrain from which the song's own image of the collective arose and sought to alter.

As discussed in the introduction, the late 1970s and early 1980s were a moment in which the desire for new forms of collective life was dammed up and the older collective way seemed damned. One would think such historical conditions would lead to more radical subjectivism in the pop anthems of the moment — Randian celebrations of unfettered laissez-faire individualism, of the I-ascendant-and-ascending. But the reverse seems true: a bumper crop of new conceptions of anthems addressing and constructing collective expressions of *we* proliferated in the period. Maybe bands thought Rush's "2112" and "Anthem" (both 1976) had left nothing else to say for the "right of the ego"? In any case, the number and variety of new *we* anthems in the period was astonishing.

Biographically, Joy Division's last single, "Love Will Tear Us Apart" (1980), deployed a collective pronoun to cover just two individuals: Ian Curtis and his wife Deborah. But the *us* of course is also Curtis and the listener, which leads the interpretation of the song down different roads to consider: Is fandom necessarily a death cult, a parasocial romance fated to wither away gradually or dramatically burn; or is the song a more ontological statement about love, the *us* meaning everyone, implying we're all doomed to love and be torn apart?

Whichever it is, the collective pronoun in this goth anthem functions to constitute a community of outsiders, positively bonded around their negative conceptions of fandom as forlorn and romantic love as tragic. As with Siouxsie and the Banshees' "Happy House" (1980), the *we* invoked here is archly mock utopian — Curtis's lovers and Siouxsie's nuclear family have been ensnared by an idealistic domestic ideology that papers over the tortures and repressions of the real thing. The *we* in these songs is those who know the darker truths that lurk beneath the surfaces — a community linked by a shared experience of lack and disconnection.

Pop anthems as disparate in sound and genre as Sister Sledge's disco perennial "We Are Family" (1979) and Ivor Cutler and Linda Hirst's recitation "Women of the World" (1983) placed a utopian faith in the power of sisterhood and the political potential of women to forge a better future:

> Women of the world take over
> Because if you don't the world will come to an end
> And we haven't got long.

These fantasy images of sisterhood and the feminine shared a vision of future liberation, either in the form of a family of sisters' "high hopes we have for the future" or as the only thing standing in the way of a (very) human-caused apocalypse. In "Women of the World," Marx and Engels's revolution credo "workers of the world unite" has been flipped into a vision of women and not industrial workers as the liberating class; in "We Are Family," the family unit is recuperated for the modest dreams of incremental progress. These are songs that locate collective power in a particular sociological unit — whether it be a new type of family or a new international gender bloc.

New euphoric conceptions of a global collective subject alternated with abject ones. From the late 1970s to early 1980s, new subjects of history stepped into legibility and audibility. Afrika Bambaataa's "Planet Rock" (1982), one of the founding blueprints for contemporary hip-hop, imagines a world united by the wild freedom of partying and a general libertinism: "No work or play, our world is free — Be what you be."

This is explicitly a utopian scenario conceived in explicitly, well, *planetary* terms: "On this Mother Earth, which is our rock," listeners are urged to escape from all rational calculus and constraint through the new medium of hip-hop. Anyone who can dance can partake in the dance. As future 2 Live Crew producer Mr. Mixx would say of the rhythmic backbone provided by the Roland TR-808 drum machine, "This is going to be the most universal machine ever."[1]

Laurie Anderson's surprise crossover hit "O Superman" (1981) conceives of collective subjectivity as a subordinate will to the military-industrial complex: a song in which the authority and control of the family, the state, and the corporation have been outsourced to a mindless, technocratic Big (M)other:

> *So hold me, Mom, in your long arms*
> *Your petrochemical arms, your military arms*
> *In your electronic arms.*

The Greek chorus of the anthemic "O Superman" and the recurring laugh, rather than representing an opposing force of grassroots democratic resistance, are equally technologically mediated and so, by the logic of the song, equally compromised: the chorus's voice has been fed through a vocoder.

This Heat managed to churn out two new dystopian points of view: the Ballardian "Fall of Saigon" (1977) and the irradiated "A New Kind of Water" (1981). In "Fall of Saigon," the *we* is represented by abandoned Western diplomats trapped in Vietnam in 1975. These characters possess solidarity but of a sordid, diabolical nature: "We ate Soda, the embassy cat" we're told in the first line. This is the unity of transnational imperialists, in this case after geopolitical defeat: "My God, we got so far" in Southeast Asia, the narrator laments, "only to eat Soda." Showing elite class solidarity to the end, the group saves the cat's choice liver for the ambassador's wife, while "for last, we saved the janitor."

If "Fall of Saigon" gives us the view from inside of a rightist cabal down-but-not-out, "A New Kind of Water" conceives of collective existence once again united, but under the hanging threat of the bad infinity brought by thermonuclear war. By the time of the 1981 album *Deceit*, This Heat was "sure we were going to die":[2]

> *Eat drink and be merry,*
> *for tomorrow we die,*
> *eat electricity.*

Before neoliberalism and neoconservatism, the proper sign of globalization was (and perhaps still is) the atomic bomb: "New York to Moscow, Nairobi in flames."

Parliament-Funkadelic's "One Nation Under a Groove" (1978), another internationalist utopian dance anthem, speaks to a more damaged political situation than one might think on first listen. As guitarist Michael Hampton put it, "I always took One Nation Under a Groove to mean that some of the world's problems are too big to change, so we might as well just groove."[3] Even the P-Funk nation's sense of communal euphoria turns its back on geopolitics, on economics, on the violence and exploitation that drive the world. In other words, this is a positive, joyous spin on the same set of collective frustrations on which This Heat and Anderson's "O Superman" put a dystopian construction.

These are the new communal images extant and circulating in the period when Bowie and Queen go into "Under Pressure": of a depoliticized global multitude sharing the bodily pleasures of music, dancing, and eroticism; nouveau would-be masters of the universe searching for solidarity in a rising technocratic military-industrial complex; and crushed, frightened, terrorized subjects of a system built for the one percent and haunted by nuclear threat. Popular anthems of the moment were exploring the micro and the macro levels of social organization and cutting out the nation-state.

The first thing to note about "Under Pressure" in this context, then, is that it projects a world without institutions. No nations, government agencies, corporations, or NGOs are mentioned. The beneficent, established institution is absent from Bowie and Mercury's vision of contemporary life. There is pressure, and there are people, and the relation between the two is not mediated by any economic, state, or non-aligned apparatus or organization.

This is not because Bowie and Queen didn't believe in the existence of institutions — joking references to "income tax" and "Watergate" pepper Queen's "Bicycle Race," and the FBI and CIA are name-checked in "The Invisible Man"; *Diamond Dogs* features enough candidates, financiers, priests, and other functionaries to populate a small town. Rather, the lack in "Under Pressure" is a symptom of 1981: anthems need institutions to celebrate, and none had any juice. There is an institution-sized hole in the song waiting to be occupied, and it soon would be, by anthems that united NGO-style global relief efforts with vague Christian undertones (e.g., "We Are the World" and "Where the Streets Have No Name").

But social relationships in "Under Pressure" are not mediated by institutions: there's only *people* under pressure. This is an anthem for a time in which there's no faith in institutions to be anything but the bearers of propaganda, crowd control, realpolitik violence, and repression. Gone were the days when anthems could believably celebrate a state, church, or even corporation's (e.g., IBM's "Ever Onward") power to catalyze peaceful relations between the one and the many, the inner and the outer.

Given this breakdown in trust, the question of who and what the people were and could be was thrown into high relief. Without institutions to create the relation between "real life" and politics, the concept and practice of mass politics was thrown into darkest night. A new image of "people" emerges in "Under Pressure" out of necessity.

But rather than plump for one new definition of the masses as defined by those on the cutting edge of the pop anthem of that moment — Parliament-Funkadelic's, Afrika Bambaataa's, Laurie Anderson's, or This Heat's — "Under Pressure" presents and articulates many dystopian and utopian conceptions of the coming community without advocating for any. Just as it abstracts the traditional requirement of the anthem to name an enemy by naming an abstraction, its conception of the "friend," the coming community, is equally innovative. It does not force on history something still in process, unavailable, and obscure.

Instead, it presents alternative visions, imagines their collisions, and waits for real, historical collectives, who may or may not be made up of the listeners, to one day give their formal skeleton the flesh and quickness of life. Bowie and Mercury spin out minimal universals — a bare-bones *we* and *us* between the poles of what Foucault was calling in 1979 the "*omnes et singulatim* [all and one]."[4] "Under Pressure" assays alternative social formations currently unavailable in practice but necessary for future survival.

As a dyad, Bowie and Mercury act out the smallest unit of collective becoming. They occupy a site of difference between the one and the many, the fantasy of the autonomous individual and the crush of the universal mass. From this vantage point, the two experiment within the social field and articulate various rhythms of togetherness that represent alternatives to the dead ends then circulating as the only possibilities: the isolated individual, autonomous but lonely, and the massive subject of the impersonal forces of our collective leviathans.

As discussed in the previous chapter, the forces of pressure in "Under Pressure" are thoroughgoing and pervasive. It would be an ahistorical exaggeration characteristic of today's ontological turn to say that Bowie and Queen claim that pressure *makes* subjects ex nihilio. Rather, in "Under Pressure" the force of power pressurize subjects — it shapes their horizons, determines their choices, and attempts to train their senses and police their moods. It is Keats's vision of "soul making" weaponized, used for social control rather than aesthetic liberation.[5] Against this, the song's form develops countervailing formulations of "people." As the pressure builds in the song, so does the intensity of its hypothetical churn of alternate forms of being, becoming and bonding, one that builds to both higher and more capacious categories and forms. This work is done, as we will see, by some tricky work with pronouns and the protean quality the of interaction between Bowie's and Mercury's singing.

The song starts with *me* and *you*: "Pressure, pushing down on me, pressing down on you." The bond here forms as subjects of a shared pressure. Because this *me* and *you* are both under pressure, they are related. This is obviously a negative but also a positive bond — a starting point for connection through a shared experience of force. In the broad strokes befitting a pop anthem, this relationship can be represented with a simple diagram: me — pressure — you. Here, pressure is the mediating force between individuals. In fact, because pressure precedes me and you in the song, it could be argued that these identities don't exist in isolation. They are given meaning and life through the actions of a mediating power. This basic mediation of social relations remains constant throughout the song: pressure both links and separates.

But *me* and *you*, like all personal pronouns, are what structural linguist Roman Jakobson calls *shifters*: their meaning changes relative to the situation in which they are communicated.[6] *I, you, he,* and the like have no inherent meaning without reference to what they describe. Bowie and Mercury, like all songwriters worth their salt, understand the built-in ambiguity in pronouns and exploit it with verve. So, when Bowie introduces the first *me,* he is already indexing several possible subject positions at once. This first-person singular pronoun is open-ended: it can be read as the biographical Bowie, the Bowie persona, the narrator of the song, an audience surrogate, and a participant observer of the life of pressure.

Likewise, the first line's *you* allows multiple positions to overlap: the biographical Mercury, the Mercury persona, the co-narrator of the song, the audience, and Bowie's partner in pressure. Whereas logical argument tends to separate and narrow these positions and identities into discrete units, "Under Pressure" begins from their imbrication in a shared field of possibility. Subject to pressure, the *me* and *you* of the song are at the outset left polyvalent, as if to facilitate the exploration of as many permutations of social linkages as possible in what follows. If it began naturalistically, the lyrics would have named the main characters and begun telling their story. But only the sketchiest outlines for couplings are provided at the start, to allow for the most capacious coordination of an anthemic subject by song's end.

Couples flit and flutter across the mind of the listener — and provide many glimpses of social relations newly available for "people" under pressure. This inductive group, "me and you," started from the ground up in the interaction between two voices and characters, is doubled by the category of general humanity, the "no man" in "no man asks for." This empty universal subject of "no man" obviously specifies a gender and so contradicts its own supposed universality at the same time it announces it. But this is a universal introduced only to be decomposed and reinvented. The double motion of the song is to build new collective forms from the outset and to decompose and specify the extant harmful models of social togetherness.

The first of these fleeting, ground-up couplings to emerge pairs Mercury the emotive worshipper with Bowie the gloomy analyst, insisting on pressure's reality principle. Formless vocables of a pop prayer ascending are checked by the downward force of a concise critical judgment. This relation, however, is not one of domination — to choose one of the pair as superior to the other misses the point. The epiphanic and interpretative approaches to pressure mirror one another; each is an attempt to escape the immediacy of its pain and regain some measure of control within the maelstrom of an overwhelming force.

Mercury seeks to flee from pressure's reaches; Bowie seeks to contain its power through the imposition of a judgment on its nature. As strategies, these approaches are linked forms of coping with the intolerable — the supplicant's escape into prayerfulness and the critic's into self-soothing judgment.

But these basic dispositions quickly glide into a new formation by the end of the verse. It's now Mercury who becomes analytical, providing a sociological snapshot: buildings are burning, and families are splitting. And after Mercury's description is complete (when houses burn, people become homeless), Bowie takes up the affective aspect, which Mercury introduced with his hymning vocables: now it's Bowie who sounds like he's squirming to escape.

Less than a minute into the song, Bowie and Mercury have already established points of view, hard-nosed analyst and spiritualist empath, *and* then exchanged these perspectives. These are useful ways to see, feel, and think in the world but are left unrooted in individual subject positions. Rather, they precede such subjects and are transferable from one person to another. When they take them on, Bowie and Mercury of course inflect these subject positions with different tones and colors, but the general dispositions are recognizable despite their singer as they recur in the anthem.

These two perspectives then meld into one. Bowie and Mercury sing the lament of the suffering: "Let me out!" Both describe witnessing friends cry out in pain, and in this moment the options of criticism and care temporarily unite. The bond between these singers is formed in the crisscrossing of POVs on a shared experience of an established social category: the friend. Just as the song begins with sketched frames for witnessing, the clinical critic, and the sentimental empath, and then complicates them by putting them into a shifting social scene, the general category of "people" begins to be specified and filled in by reference to "friend," which is both general (in Whodini's "how many of us have them?" sense) and specific to the singers' particular friends.

Here it's important to remember that the catastrophe of the song's beginning, the breakup of livable space (burning buildings) and the family unit, also makes it possible to imagine new spaces and social bonds. It is at once a tragedy and an opening. In the wake of this going to pieces, new social forms must rise.

Yet at this point, a gulf still separates the Mercury-Bowie couple, both distanced observers of the suffering of others, the worst victims of postmodernity's pressure, whether the true wretched of the earth or the singers' own suicidal friends. Mercury and Bowie are compositing a compound vision, a pair of at first divergent witnesses; at the same time, they are tying together unknown, imagined suffering "people" with their "good friends."

The two have yet to be linked but are being brought nearer to one another.

In fact, after this momentary closing of the gap between Mercury and Bowie, between intimates ("good friends") and abstract strangers ("people"), there's something of a "refusal of the call": Mercury's character retreats from the scene of conflict into the security of solipsistic reverie. The considerations of friends and "people" in extremis disappear, and a figure of idle escape, the only in the song, enters. Mercury's character aimlessly kicks "his brains 'round the floor" and inadequately sums up the situation with a when-it-rains-it-pours shrug.

But this escape is illusory. Mercury quickly is on to something else. The verse's strange image of Mercury kicking his brains across the floor starts as a metaphor for idle distraction but becomes a grotesque figure for the externalization of inner thought and feeling. Even the brain, the classical symbol of inwardness, has a life outside the body here. Combined with the stock visual of pouring rain, one gets the very odd image of an exposed brain in a downfall. Whether or not this was Mercury's intention, they produce this bizarre possibility through juxtaposition. It is the sort of image Bowie the Dada follower would have relished mixing into a pop anthem. As the mechanical metaphor implies, pressure here tends to force insides out.

While the sound and tone are definitely Queen's in this moment, we also hear Mercury's position shading toward Bowie's: the mind becomes a brain as subjectivity is momentarily turned inside out and concretized into an object for listeners. And while there is some agency represented here (Mercury's still doing the kicking), it is an action made under duress.

Then comes Mercury's attack on another cliché: "It never rains but it pours." Now this might not approach the zenith of lyric poetry, but it works the theme and again finds an external, collectively shared figure for private, internal states of mind. Nothing's more banal than talking about the weather and nothing's more common. And here, the metaphor functions as a down-to-earth sharable figure, much like pressure: it is a phrase between dead metaphor and alien neologism.

Béla Tarr supposedly once said that in Andrei Tarkovsky's films, rain purifies, but in his own it just makes mud. In "Under Pressure," rain does neither—it represents neither Christian salvation nor a token of naturalistic fatality. If there is hope, it is for people, whatever they might be, and the many ways they may come into being through social experience, not from Tarkovsky's divine or Tarr's ruthless reduction of rain to a non-symbol, a literal, dumb mechanism good only for making miserable mud.

In the next verse, Mercury rejects both transcendence and nihilism for the more modest prerogative of a witness: "Sat on a fence, but it don't work." While Bowie's character keeps being frozen out by the paralyzing terror of too much sympathy, Mercury's fence-sitting persona has been too aloof and impassive to feel much of anything one way or another: he has been a disengaged, idle spectator. The point is that both normative approaches to the suffering of others lead to the same lack of action: Bowie's liberal and Mercury's libertine bystanders, despite their differing emotional weather, terminate in the same quietism.

Considering Bowie and Mercury were two of the most famous bisexual/queer figures of the early eighties (and most likely shared a brief sexual relationship in the early seventies), it's tempting to think about fence-sitting as a metaphor for gender fluidity. If Mercury's fence-sitting metaphor is an allusion to his and/or Bowie's queerness, however, it is quite a tamped-down one. In any case, in "Under Pressure" the fence is not a place to rest contentedly, let alone a still point in the turning world. Like gender identity and erotic desire, it is just one locale in a vast and complicated cosmos of pressure and its network of social relations. One must eventually get off the fence in "Under Pressure," not only because decisions must be made and actions taken but because the space of indeterminacy and fluid liminality represented by the fence is just one possible affective position among many others, and it's not always the most strategically important or useful one.

If Bowie and Mercury momentarily establish erotic bonds in "Under Pressure," they are faint and transitory—erotic coupling never dominates the many forms of social being experimented with in the song. Desire, including a queer-oriented desire, is neither suppressed nor dwelt on. This is in keeping with the form of the pop anthem, which seeks both to do justice to the multiplicity of possibility within the social body *and yet* let no one become central and dominant. A pop anthem cannot risk the whole for any one part, yet it remains unbelievable if it does not touch the manifold social parts that make up the whole. "The fence" in this song, therefore, neither represents nor excludes so-called "bisexual epistemologies": connection based on erotic desire, even if "transgressive," is only one version of sociality, not the utopian model for the coming community. There is never a sense that queer desire alone could solve the world's structural contradictions. In "Under Pressure," the means of connection between individuals and groups — analysis, empathy, desire, immersion, and love — are not the exclusive possessions of any one identity, even if specific forms of sociality start within these identity formations.

And it's the anthem form that explains the transformation of pronouns and proper names from the song's early demo to its final release. In the early demo, most glaringly, there are characters! Vignettes feature Mercury chatting with a lady "sitting on the stage," Brian May singing of "silent and lonely" street urchins with "nowhere to run," and Bowie invoking the sight of a not-yet-proverbial "blind man" to claim even he "could see" New York City is not the hell it's sometimes made out to be.

Near the demo's end, Bowie even allows himself a personal pronoun in the form of an illocutionary command: it is not "love dares us" (as in the final) but "*I* dare *you* to care for the people on the edge of the night" and Bowie himself (not "love") that "dares you" to "change your [not "our"] way of caring about ourselves."

The more concrete characters and familiar pronoun-verb-object sentence structures of the rough draft give the song more of a clear narrative, albeit still only an outline. But they take away from its anthemic call to an unrestricted audience.

In the final version, New Yorkers have become general citizens of the world, allowing Mercury's and Bowie's characters themselves to be folded ultimately into their number. In the early version, individual characters act. In the final version, what matters is not individual characters and types but the bonding actions and concepts between them in living relation.

A brief digression — around this time in his career, Bowie expressed a wish to "come in touch with a common factor" by making "probably the simplest music I've ever done."[7] A soft repudiation of his bisexual past in *Rolling Stone*, the slick simplicity of the album *Let's Dance*, a daft Pepsi commercial, the gormless "Dancing in the Street" video, *Labyrinth*, and worse were to come as the eighties rolled on. Because "Under Pressure" inaugurated this period of a more front-facing, artistically compromising and compromised Bowie, it would be easy to read the song retroactively as the beginning of a long slide for Bowie. The song, after all, stands between the avant pop brilliance of *Scary Monsters (and Super Creeps)* (1980) and the high-selling but safe *Let's Dance* (1983). But if the song sits on another fence — the one between experimental and the poptomistic commercialism of Bowie's middling-to-terrible 1980s — "Under Pressure" is better understood as a one-off, an unstable mixture that captured a stunning collision of styles, modes, and contents and harnessed them into a hit single but proved irreproducible.

Never again would Bowie so successfully skate the edge between avant obscurantism and an AstroTurf corporate populism stuck in the middle of the road. After "Under Pressure," Bowie would spend much of his time oscillating between creating music for an abstract mass of "people" as consumers or lost in fragmentary, barely expressive explorations of those "small universes that can be created in the mind."[8] In other words, Bowie would rarely again (and not consistently until 2016's *Blackstar*) manage to believably relate the pronouns *I* and *we* in a convincing and interesting fashion. Collaborating with Queen, a group always producing with mass audiences in mind, forced Bowie to adapt, and this rare experimental populist work was the result.

For Mercury, fence-sitting is synonymous with denial of the political, a flight from crisis and its attendant suffering: "Turned away from it all / like a blind man." Remembering that Bowie initially sang "even the blind man could see that's not so [that New York City is dangerous]" in the demo, the change to Mercury's released version is better in every way. Not only is it detached from any one individual's point of view, it is also now a hinge image, a prelude to action: an anticipation of a jump *off* the fence.

This, beyond having the salutary effect of invoking disability in less invidious terms, eliminates Mercury's personal pronoun in the fashion of Bowie's earlier practice. This is the last hit of Mercury's more individually, personally minded lyric, but shorn of its

subject pronouns, it's also a transition to the collective deperson-
alization of the song's incipient twin climaxes: Freddie's soaring
plea that we "give love one more chance" and Bowie's vertiginous
concluding dive into the risks and dangers of what "love dares
us" to do. It's as if only when individual subjectivity, in both its
comforts and hardships, has been exposed as insufficient can
the song start discussing its positive term, love.

The introduction of love as potential counterforce to pressure
inaugurates the song's first invocation of the first-person plural:
we, us, our. "Under pressure *we're* cracking," Bowie sings the first
time love is mentioned, and soon "love," like pressure, terror, and
insanity in the song, is given dominion over human affairs: now
"love," not Bowie's "I," takes action, and it gives the exhortation
to all persons to dare to care. The various subject positions have
coalesced into a provisional collective aggregate.

But what is the content of this communal, potentially planetary subject of love? It is deducible only by the qualities its bearers embody: a force committed rather than indifferent (con-
tra the fence-sitting of the previous verse), an antidote to total
breakdown and to the insanity and "cracking" produced by pressure, a form of communal self-love (to care about ourselves), and
a dare to care for others ("the people on the edge of the night"). It
is a force of change and transformation. The individuals and collectives that embody this kind of love must be mutable, open, and
willing to struggle for an equality never yet practiced on earth,
and must be focused on the process of struggle, not obsessed

with hope for future victory or fear of defeat. One could criticize the vagueness and lack of concrete political solutions offered by this position, but to me what the song does is quite magical: it leaves open a position for a future community and adumbrates only the minimal features of a community needed for love to win for the first time.

In doing so, it dodges identifying "the people" with the proletariat (or any other class), the family, nation, or certain individuals; it avoids reducing "people" to the voluntaristic delusions of the anarchist and avant-gardist camp, or the citizens of a particular state or corporation; neither does it define love in mystical realms of removal from earth and its material problems. In a time when all collective action was frozen and compromised, when the available social bonds were either violent or withered, the song provides a loose framework for people (i.e., listeners) to fill with their own action until better conditions arise. This may seem like not enough, but anything more explicit can only be found in a manifesto, on the march, or in battle.

One more thing remains stunning about Bowie and Mercury's shared performance. Even as the song reaches a crescendo and a collective subject emerges, there's no sense that the two voices and two points of view ever fuse without remainder. While both move from outside witnesses to participant observers, and while the song's vision of shared struggle articulates a people, it never becomes the gray totalitarian (or consumerist clone) crowd in which all difference is submerged in uniform fealty to authority. Although Bowie and Mercury find a place in the crowd in the shared risk of abandoning voyeurism for "love," they never stop contending with one another: difference and multiplicity are preserved within their collective vision. It *is* their collective vision.

This manifests most tellingly in the fact that this song of collective togetherness features not one but two separate climaxes: Mercury's 1960s question — Why can't we give love one more chance?, with his ecstatic echoing cries of the word "love" — on the one hand and, on the other, Bowie's hard-nosed definition of love as a daring force antagonistic to the dominant ways of the world ca. 1981. Even when love becomes the shared force connecting the singers, their visions and tones maintain some distance, only ever partially overlapping.

Between the antisocial isolation of the amatory couple and the pure public submission of the self to the norms of the crowd demanded as much by Reagan's state as, say, General Wojciech Jaruzelski's in Poland, "Under Pressure" uneasily articulates a third relation between the one and the many. This relation is called love, and love in the song is the struggle and risk to stay committed rather than nihilistic, to generate new social formations even when they seem impossible to imagine. When everyone is "withdrawn" and "split up," as laments a minor character in Krzysztof Kieslowski's *No End* (set during the 1981 repression of the Solidarity movement in Poland), even minor tenderness is everywhere threatened.

This is the unpropitious land from which Bowie and Mercury model multiple possible forms of a loving relation — witness and sufferer, critic and subject, politically committed and libertine, lover and loved. The people in "Under Pressure" are something yet to be made out of the sort of social relations modeled by Bowie and Mercury's series of couplings, latent and so imaginable but blocked from practice by the system's pressure.

▶ 03 Streets

AT SOME POINT LATE in the twentieth century, people stopped assuming the street and the "streets" were the locus for the eruption of the new and revolutionary into the world. Periodization is always an imprecisely dated affair, but it does seem that a wide variety of modernity's master thinkers assumed the centrality of the city street until when? 1945? 1968? 1972? In the nineteenth century, Karl Marx assumed revolutions would kick off where modernization had reached the point of maximum contradiction — megalopolises like Berlin and Paris. Georg Simmel implicitly argued in "The Metropolis and Mental Life" that urban experience was more advanced, because it was more adapted to shock, than rural experience.[1]

The police and the forces of "law and order" agreed and wanted to control city populations through the management of space. The history of the street is also the history of Haussmannization in Paris to prevent revolutionary organization and revolt; the construction of a surveillance state with CCTV, drones, phones, and helicopters; the infiltration of leftist and countercultural organizations; and everything from the development of professional sociology to the militarization of police forces. Architecture and space by 1981 were certainly no longer (if they had ever been) politically neutral backdrops for history. Marxist theoreticians and fellow travelers were the first to point this out, but now it's increasingly taken for granted.

Tracing a line from Henri Lefebvre's conception of "abstract space" in 1974 to Marc Augé's "non-places" in 1992 and on through to Rem Koolhaas's "generic city" in 1997, we can follow the deepening realization that at various scales, urban space has been produced to maintain the status quo and block radical action. Abstract, generic non-places are concepts for a world of controlled streets, no longer openings to mass action. Gentrification, surveillance, and militarized policing usually enforce their seeming opposite, the calm of a pacified zone, repetitive, delocalized, and tedious spaces where nothing new seems possible. Today, no one street ever connects to the beating heart of capital. Every street seems a capillary, one as relatively insignificant as the next, in a system without a central artery. Like finance, the physical world is now a system without a center and has no vital street addresses.

How did the meaning of the street shift so radically? Partially, it was because as content, the "streets" themselves, as argued above, had themselves changed in political, social, and aesthetic character. For a tradition of modernist music that needed the streets to be exciting, rockers seemed to find either flat despair or blank, affectless coping by denizens of the contemporary street. Seemingly only a fool could read "Streets of the Lost" (1983) in

Life or watch the documentary that followed it, *Streetwise* (1984), on homeless pre-teens and teens in Seattle, and write an old-fashioned anthem.

Modernism had always been a movement of the cities: a channeling and abstraction of street energy, whether Vorticist London or Bauhaus Berlin, post-Impressionist Paris, Futurist Rome, and so on. Walter Benjamin turned to Charles-Pierre Baudelaire's poetry in response to Paris as the most cutting-edge take on capitalist culture. Rock and roll, despite its sometimes location in the suburban garage and provincial backwater, was predominantly city music.

When Lou Reed name-checks "Lexington 125" or Bob Dylan "4th Street," it was with an insouciant confidence that New York City streets were the center of the countercultural universe. The participants of May 1968, in poetic slogans graffitied on the walls of Paris dreaming of finding the beach under the cobblestones, assumed the same — that the city street is the fulcrum from which the masses could change the world. It was absolutely accepted that cities were where the most advanced artistic techniques, concepts, and movements were born and took root first.

The street, too, had long been considered the site of what Barbara Ehrenreich termed "collective joy": her history of such joy, after all, is titled *Dancing in the Streets*, after the Martha and the Vandellas' 1964 anthem.[2] Symptomatically, Bowie and Mick Jagger would photocopy "Dancing in the Street" for a lifelessly bad cover in 1985.

The theorist Mikhail Bakhtin's *Rabelais and His World* celebrated the world turned upside down and the subversions of hierarchy that occur during carnival, where everyday people acted out utopian fantasies in eruptions of anarchic desire. This was the joy of the multitude, and until fairly late into the twentieth century, the streets were taken for granted as the catalyst and setting for such joy's springing forth. The street was the stage where the highs and lows of modernity's melodrama was assumed to play out.

What had changed by 1981? Well, successful twentieth-century revolutions had kicked off far from the streets of Berlin and Paris, most dramatically in largely agrarian Russia and China, and were rural revolutions. Post-1945, new forms of delocalization and decentralization altered the situation of the city street. The nuclear bomb meant all streets were equal under its destructive eye — all equally annihilable, and therefore not inherently special or essential to the world order. Finance capital, with its increasingly cloistered abstraction from the "real world" of street-level commodity exchange, meant that business could happen anywhere, or nowhere, virtually. Becoming more and more fictional, the flows of capital meant that "the streets" and any given real street become of much less importance. Meanwhile, flight to the suburbs and newer zones of exurban sprawl meant fewer people experienced the city at all, except behind windshields or briefly on walks from subway to office.

Due in large part to neoliberal attacks on the welfare state and the very notion of social insurance, city streets in the late 1970s and 1980s became avenues of the damned, thoroughfares of bombed-out urban hollows rather than vibrant vortices of public life. In places like New York City, a test case for the new neoliberal financial policy, new art temporarily thrived "Downtown"—Jean-Michel Basquiat and no wave in clubs like the Mudd Club and the Kitchen—but these proved temporary florescences, performances in the seams of a larger destruction.

In this time, metropolitan life in New York City had become so vicious, no one looked to it as a laboratory of the future anymore. Things were so bad even hippie mystic Cat Stevens felt compelled to stay strapped: on 1978's "New York Times," Mr. "Peace Train" himself lamented that "you need a gun to walk into New York." If the city street was no longer the center of the political and aesthetic universe, that it was just a blighted dead zone appeared a very real possibility. European cities were often no better than the Big Apple: when Bowie and Iggy Pop fled to Berlin to kick drugs in 1976, they were amazed to find themselves in the heroin capital of the late twentieth century.

So, by 1981, Bowie and Queen must have been wondering about the fate of the street as they wrote and recorded a song originally titled "People on Streets." In 2013, Bowie would write a languorous lament for the old *Strasse* of Berlin entitled "Where Are We Now?," but he and Queen were already asking the question in

1981. In fact, they had been doing so since the early 1970s, both in their music and in their personal lives. If the metropolitan city street was no longer where the newest developments in radical politics and cutting-edge art could be found and produced, what role did "the street" now have in the pop anthem?

In non-pop anthems, the setting must transcend the local particulars of its inspiration. This is because the song must speak in mythic tones for a broad community: If the "The Star-Spangled Banner" were laden with too many references to the Battle of Fort McHenry and Baltimore, the vaunting feel would be grounded and the majority of America's population alienated or confused. In the "Marine's Hymn," Mexico is elevated to "the Halls of Montezuma." In the Vietnamese revolutionary anthem "March to the Front," the actual street settings for demonstrations and anticolonial guerrilla warfare become "the long and arduous road."

Unlike pop music, littered with references to and descriptions of real streets, the pop anthem did not deviate from its genre convention. The actual, concrete, physical location must be sublated into something grander if it is going into an anthem. While the cities of "Black America" are extensively name-checked in "Dancing in the Street," not a single real street, avenue, or drive is mentioned. And in "Under Pressure," the streets of New York City in the demo became the more general "streets" in the final.

Bowie's relation to the street was always askew: he is much more often a watcher and observer of street life than an active participant. Down to the last song of his last LP, *Blackstar*'s "I Can't

Give Everything Away" (2016), he insisted on his powers of withdrawn spectatorship as the core of his art:

Seeing more and feeling less
Saying "No" but meaning "Yes"
This is all I ever meant.

On "Queen Bitch" (1971), he's "watching the cruisers below" from the "eleventh floor." In a song heavily lyrically and musically indebted to the Velvet Underground's "I'm Waiting for the Man," Bowie's revision lies primarily in this shift in point of view away from the street level of Lou Reed's "Lexington 125" to one above the fray.

On *Diamond Dogs*, the streets are dystopian slums with stage-managed Potemkin village avenues. Bowie's POV slides from fascist designer of these streets to just another of its denizens. By the time of *"Heroes,"* Bowie has become a wholly passive victim of the streets. In "Blackout," set during the New York City blackout of 1977, a hysterically voiced Bowie spends half of the song horizontal, blacked out from drink and drugs, begging bystanders to "get me to the doctor!," "get me on my feet!," and "get me off the streets!" Tellingly, his character is too disoriented to report any particulars of the local color (also, there's no light). Yet despite his constant self-distancing POV in the songs, biographically (and like Mercury) he was very much an active participant out "in these streets" (at least until his marriage to Iman in 1992), sleeping with men and women, frequently on the search for sex and drugs.

As discussed in the previous chapter, at the time of recording "Under Pressure," David Bowie and Freddie Mercury were arguably the most famous queer musicians, maybe humans, in the world. And while both seemed to have the same libidinous approach to street life, Bowie tended to play himself up as a pansexual libertine in the press, while Freddie kept his private doings with sex and drugs on the low. His sexual orientation, of course, was something of an open secret in those times, given his campy performances and flamboyant outfits: the sequined jumpsuits of the mid-seventies and the leather daddy and Castro clone fits of the late seventies and early eighties scanned as anything but heterosexual. Just like Bowie, Mercury was torn between immersion in the hedonistic demimonde of the city street and a need to observe it from a distance: "Mercury adored New York. It was a city he would often roam, exploring especially its seedier sides. He also enjoyed visiting the numerous gay clubs and bars, and loved to cruise the streets at night in a darkened limousine. From the car he surveyed the parade of street life, sipping on his favourite iced vodka."[3] And though Mercury's lyrics usually kept the raunch to a minimum and his sexual orientation highly encrypted under allegorical forms, "Under Pressure" actually started as a paean to cruising. Queen's demo for "Feel Like," which originates the rhythmic rudiments and basic guitar pattern of "Under Pressure," tells a story from the perspective of a guy attempting to seduce a man he passes on the street: "I see you walking with that other guy / I see your face, you're not satisfied," Mercury announces. Soon, he's piling on come-on after come-on, ending with "I wanna be there, in that truck." This is as explicitly erotic as Mercury's lyrics would ever get, showing the difference between the sensibility he shared in a semiprivate rehearsal and the one on Queen's official releases.

Bowie and Mercury both felt this push and pull of the street, defined by a twinned, contradictory desire for opposed terms of experience: immersion and spectatorship, fucking and critical judgment, the raw presentation of real life and the need to re-present it. In other words, before "Under Pressure" and the 1980s, the streets in the songs of Bowie and Queen were recognizably modern and modernist: the streets were the source of the real and the place of its transformation into art and entertainment; the brothels of modernism; the "pornosophical philotheology" of James Joyce's "Nighttown"; immersion in the flesh and its extraction into an artistic and conceptual form.[4] In other words, slumming and objectification of "the streets" morphed into a more rarefied form of art and discourse.

But as argued above, by "Under Pressure" it was no longer certain that the street was the fulcrum for radical transformations in politics, aesthetics, and everyday life. As such, the constitutive tension that animated modernist pop music even in the sixties and seventies had slackened. The streets were not essential to experience living history anymore — they were now just another place. People of course continued and (still continue) to slum, and to mine their visits to "the streets" for their own writing and art, but there's no sense that the work that comes out of it is at the center of the postmodern experience. By 1981, there was nothing central to history or particularly fascinating about life on the street.

Which is perhaps why with every revision of "Under Pressure," both libidinal desire and street-level observation are more refined out of it. Both the joy and squalor of "the streets" (the *nostalgie de la boue*) are replaced with a world in which streets are almost blank and impossible to romanticize. For modernist rock music that is, the old conception of the streets had lost its savor, and musicians were wondering what came next.

By 1981 in rock, the former paradigm of music as inherently *street* was exhausted. The contradictory, vexed vortex of desire, immersion, and creation in the city demimonde no longer struck a chord — when counterculture luminaries like Lou Reed returned to it on records like *Street Hassle* (1978) and *The Blue Mask* (1982), it was often embarrassing and strange, an outdated transmission from a past world of glamour in the gutter. Nascent genres, rap first and foremost but electro and boogie as well, were producing a new street imaginary in sync with the present situation, but pop and rock's "street music" seemed almost spent by the early 1980s.

The pop anthem was left with the empty street. Formerly a site where the universal could be gleaned from the particular, the street was now either an abstract, generic non-site or a purely local space of no broader interest to the world at large. It was as if the circuit had been shorted between the real street and the imaginary one. If the setting of the pop anthem was missing in action, and the street was just so much tarmac, concrete, and paint, no longer a believable fulcrum from the actual to the mythopoetic and epiphanic, clearly something had to be done. In 1981, William Gibson coined the phrase "the street finds its own uses for things."[5] The reverse was also true of this historical moment: to stay alive, musicians in a variety of genres (mostly non-rock) were also in the process of finding their own uses for the streets.

If the old anthems romanced local streets into epic, even sacred spaces, new pop anthems would have to do something else. This happened across a variety of genres — in electro funk and roots rock, crossover Islands pop and D-beat. Cybotron's first single, "Alleys of Your Mind" (1981), prepared the table for all techno to follow and, as its title suggests, shuns the main road for the backstreets. This change in location is also a change in tone: the alleys in the song are a psychogeographic production of a Vietnam veteran returned to his hometown of Detroit from the "barren land" of war.

The song, like the album *Clear* as a whole, is a stunning premonition of virtual life: the intensification of simulated space at the expense of the built world. These alleys of the mind are obscure and encrypted, and so isolate the narrator from participation in society at large: "Paranoia right behind alleys of your mind / out of sync, out of rhyme." The physical alleys of Detroit ca. 1981 are dematerialized and turned inside out: what's important are the convoluted byways of the narrator's psyche. The alleys of Detroit have become a metaphor for the singer's inner space: wherever he goes, this interior geography abides within him, dominating his perception.

A cryptic, elliptical network of thoughts and feelings happen away from the main roads of modern life. The singer is trapped inside himself, lost in one alley after another. The vocals are mixed low and delivered with a regimented syncopation. The alleys of the mind are not sentimental, filled with the pathos of the ruined castle of World War I shell-shock victims: the singing and the looping "electronics" provided by Juan Atkins and Richard Davis suggest the damaged psyche itself has been automated.

The alleys of the mind are not the material connectors of a living neighborhood community; the song is an anthem not for a broad, pop following looking for escapism but necessarily a niche audience willing to take a journey into the headspace of a damaged, manipulated, and paranoid subject. While the song cannot dispense with the concept of literal space entirely, it lingers on only as a figure for an inner world made by war trauma, automation, and alienation.

Bruce Springsteen is well known as a chronicler and celebrant of street life in New York and New Jersey. His first LP, after all, is called *Greetings from Asbury Park, N.J.* and spins out one verbose urban tableau after another. His characters are constantly out on the avenues, bridges, and expressways of the Northeast, cruising in Chevys and on Harleys, through Junglelands and on Thunder Roads. This became such an established part of his shtick that when Bob Dylan and Tom Petty wanted to parody Springsteen on "Tweeter and the Monkey Man," they simply had to lard the song with as many of Springsteen's place-names (real and parodic) as possible.

On these streets, the real American, both mythopoetic and down to earth, could be found. Here was the essential setting for Springsteen's epic Americana, the heart of a seemingly heartless nation. Main Street USA, 1950s-style, was beyond the pale for Springsteen as a setting for a nationalist anthem after, say, Vietnam (an obsession he shared with Cybotron), so albums like *Born to Run* tried instead to reinvigorate the backstreets of one region and make that stand for the authentic American spirit. It's almost as if, given the failure of the American project writ large, Springsteen returns to a dream of the city-state, with Jersey City as his Athens.

Even on a record titled *Nebraska*, recorded in the last month of 1981 and released in 1982, Springsteen can't quit the streets of Jersey: there is "Atlantic City," "Johnny 99" takes place in Bergen County, the eponymous "Mansion on the Hill" is in Linden, Joe Roberts in "Highway Patrolman" works in Perryville, "State Trooper" is set on the New Jersey Turnpike, and so on. By contrast, the street settings outside of this region are generic and secondhand, bare references to the names of highways and interstates. The title song's Midwestern and Western particulars are heavily cribbed from Terrence Malick's *Badlands*.

The similarity between the Clash's engaged street songs on *Sandinista!* (1980), the poles of which are represented by "Somebody Got Murdered" and "Washington Bullets," and Eddy Grant's Islands pop smash "Electric Avenue" (1982) may seem superficial, basically limited to a shared time period. But both engage with and reenact scenes of actual street violence, refashioning them for public consumption.

"Somebody Got Murdered" relates the death of an American parking attendant stabbed over a few dollars; "Electric Avenue" makes explicit reference to the Brixton riots (compare the Clash's "The Guns of Brixton") and 1981's "short hot summer" of Black anti-police uprisings that roiled England. "Washington Bullets" is a cursory world-systems map of imperialism, an indictment of not only US-backed violence in Jamaica, Chile, and Cuba but also Russian war against the Taliban (a take that hasn't aged all that well), Chinese domination of Tibet, and British war profiteering.

So, the subject matter of Eddy Grant and the Clash are surprisingly similar. But the way they deal with setting, the way they map scenes of popular uprising and state violence, are obviously quite different. It would be easy to name the Clash as the sophisticated good guys preaching militancy and analysis and Grant as the superfluous would-be pop star cheapening real history for a one-hit wonder. "Washington Bullets" has inspired articles and books from serious leftist historians Greg Grandin and Vijay Prashad; "Electric Avenue," while an undeniable jam, has produced no such intellectual lineage.

Rather than play a game of musical heroes and villains, it's more interesting to consider *Sandinista!* and "Electric Avenue" as two divergent interventions into the crisis of space and place. In other words, they are two parts of the same system. They are both aesthetic answers to the feelings of the new placelessness of the built world — its inability to become what David Harvey would too sanguinely call "spaces of hope" for artists, egalitarians, and revolutionaries alike.[6] Both the Clash and Eddy Grant visualize counter-spaces in song because they are lacking in real life.

In "Washington Bullets," Joe Strummer provides a skeletal schema of geopolitical pain points, but in a slightly pedantic, po-faced fashion unremedied by the song's jaunty xylophone and slightly arch vocal delivery. "Somebody Got Murdered," on the contrary, draws interest because it deals with a single incident of street crime and touches down with the brutal particulars where the flesh of a single gruesomely slaughtered person meets the road:

> *His name cannot be found*
> *A small stain on the pavement*
> *They'll scrub it off the ground.*

While "Washington Bullets" surveys and snapshots the streets of global imperialism, "Somebody Got Murdered" stays with one crime at the World's End Housing Estate off the Kings Road in West London. *Sandinista!* alternates between such microscopy and macro-analysis, compelling aesthetically and preaching politically.

In their anthems, they alternate between drawing political maps and painting scenes of individual action, struggle, and suffering. The generalized streets of "Washington Bullets" remain separate from the patch of bloody housing estate pavement of "Somebody Got Murdered." One street can no longer find a way to universal representation, nor can a general vision account for the singular textures of any personal street.

"Electric Avenue," of course, takes a different route: one could enjoy listening to it a hundred times in a row and never connect it to the anti-police Brixton riots of April 1981. The San Fernando teens of the 1983 film *Valley Girl* drink and dance to "Electric Avenue" at a house party, and the song's "politics" don't register for the characters or the viewer one bit.

This is not so much a song about the riots as a citation of them, and an extended fantasia inspired as much by the street name "Electric Avenue" as the contemporary history that it had recently witnessed. This is both the song's failing and its strength: it is fun and exciting in a way the Clash attempt to achieve on "Washington Bullets" (i.e., the lighthearted vibraphone) but do not quite succeed. As a political treatise, it is platitudinous, even generic, compared to *Sandinista!*'s sharpest moments, but the virtual street the music creates is vital and vibrant in a way the diagrammatic settings of "Washington Bullets" are not. It's as if the street can be unique, novel, and thrilling or soberly represented politically, but not both at once.

Two new genres ca. 1981, D-beat hardcore (sometimes called street punk) and rap, represent the intensification of this problem. This makes intuitive sense, considering hardcore and rap themselves are heightened responses to first-wave punk and reggae toasting, themselves (as we have seen) already thematically and formally centered on representing and reinventing the street. The differences are instructive. On Discharge's "Does This System Work," the old centrality of the street is preserved, but at the expense of all its old potentials and variety.

In a reinvention of the late nineteenth century's grim naturalism, the street spells misery and doom for its denizens: the setting is unspecified because the roadways where "men and women young and old" are "out on the streets homeless" could be anywhere on the globe, in Discharge's native Britain or somewhere on this "planet of slums." The street here is universal in a wholly negative way: its misery can be found globally. The songs' "plastic bag . . . homes," rags passing as clothes, and dumpster diving for a "dog end" has an implied setting that is everywhere and nowhere in particular. The music, a punishing advance on and distillation of first-wave punk, bludgeons the listener with its righteous rage but provides no liberal silver linings to the situation it diagnoses. Discharge's is the anti-carnivalesque street:

the festival is over, and trash is all that is left in the road. Ironically, because cultural studies often lagged behind its popular "objects" (e.g., street punk records) in complexity and sophistication, the carnivalesque was just being "rediscovered," celebrated, and applied in Anglo-American humanities departments (Bakhtin's *The Dialogic Imagination* was republished in English in 1981 and *Rabelais and His World* in 1984).

Melle Mel and Grandmaster Flash's "The Message," in contrast, presents a hybrid vision of life on the street. Whereas the song shares much of the fundamental critique of "Does This System Work" (albeit with an anticipation of Stuart Hall's formula "race as the modality in which class is lived"), it aesthetically works much differently than Discharge's brief blast of sheer rejection.[7]

Because it is a chronicle of specific social ills "in the ghetto," from decrepit living conditions to sexual exploitation, rampant street crime, and police brutality, and features vignettes with allegorical character sketches (the narrator, "a crazy lady," a sex worker tagged a "Zircon princess," the narrator's brother and son, Betty and her mother, a few cops, etc.), it opens itself up as a spectacle of Black street life for the general audience of radio listeners and MTV viewers. Melle Mel and Duke Bootee's generally harsh reportage is leavened by its singsong delivery, Grandmaster Flash's infectious the Whole Darn Family sample, and the song's occasional dip into rhyme-happy lyrics ("Sometimes I think I'm going insane / I swear I might hijack a plane").

Although the song is rightly considered one of the most significant in hip-hop history, one of the first serious pieces of rap social commentary and a departure from the pure party vibes of disco rap, it also contains this opening to mass consumer voyeurism. The street is figured as a real space of impoverished Black suffering and a virtual space of enjoyment for consumers of the unrestricted audience of the international cultural industry. Phil Collins, for one, was immediately inspired by the entertaining novelty of "The Message," cribbing the song's iconic "Ha ha ha ha" laugh for 1983's Genesis single "Mama." The street in popular music could be unrelentingly portrayed as politically and socially miserable, the same everywhere, as in Discharge; or it could be portrayed as a variegated dark carnival, still teeming with damaged but vital life. The streets on "The Message" have been irradiated, filled with an energy that can also kill.

"Under Pressure" conceptualizes the streets of contemporary life differently. The dark Americana of *Nebraska* is still too much of a nationalist mythology for it, just with the value signs swapped from positive to negative. The uniformly malign global street of Discharge is self-serious and doesn't do justice to the obvious fact that even by the late date of 1981, all streets around the world are not quite identical and still vary from situation to situation. This even though capitalism and its vision of space had indeed penetrated every corner of the globe. "Under Pressure" also avoids the Clash's programmatic agitprop about the streets.

Nor is the street the scene for a carnivalesque pop neutralization of historical crisis, as with the catchy and fun "Electric Avenue," where the happy-go-lucky music and identikit "protest" lyrics neutralize the actual acts of rioting, uprising, and state violence of England 1981 on which it's based. One suspects that had the song been a Queen solo project, perhaps this is the direction "Under Pressure" might have taken.

The street of "Under Pressure" is closest to the urban "jungle" described in "The Message." In both, the street means exposure of the previously protected insides — of subjectivity, of dwelling, of private life — to bombardment by public violence, "social" disease, police oppression, and repression, all the anomie effects that stem from a situation in which all but the rich few are abandoned by state and corporation.

And as in "The Message," the city street is still an important scene for the most modern symptoms of contemporary life and the lever for real and not simply spectacular resistance to the system. But "Under Pressure" does not locate the heart of such social reading and pushback in New York City (although in the first draft it did). Unlike "The Message," the song is not reported from the perspective of a street-dwelling New Yorker.

So, the streets in "Under Pressure" are not fitted into a vision of a larger urban jungle, cage, grid, maze, map, carnival, or high-

way system. Instead, the setting of "Under Pressure" is international but variable from one place to the next, potentially liber-
atory *and* a space of doom. What's important is that the streets
here are shapers of thought, affect, and physical action, not inert
containers for activity. If no single metropolitan street was any
longer the center of the system, and streets in general were emp-
tier or crueler than they once were, for Bowie and Queen they
still play a vital function in contemporary life. They help produce
and expose the state of contemporary contradictions: they are a
diagnostic tool from which the symptoms, signs, and wonders of
present life can be measured against the past's.

This approach manifests itself in the form of the song by the
way in which the street produces various narrative focalizations,
ways of looking. Rather than plump for one ultimate point of
view, Bowie and Mercury test the strengths and weaknesses of
various "street views" with the hope of finding one that can work
for the moment. The first of these potential narrative points of
view is the eye-to-eye, face-to-face view.

In the demo for "Under Pressure," Freddie sings about being
"one and one with people on streets," but this intimate, leveling
POV is nowhere to be found in the final version. This street-level
relation is explicitly contrasted with Bowie's lines that follow
(also elided from the final release): "You count them in figures /
I call them friends." So in the song's early stages, there's a contrast between a Whitmanesque celebration of immersion in the

intimate, face-to-face democracy of the streets of New York and a position Bowie holds up for scorn, which dehumanizes individuals by treating them as statistics.

So why was this direct contrast removed from the song? Because the street described in "Under Pressure" does not allow an easy, sentimental ethical opposition between good, kind individual relationships and evil views of populations and collectives. Both of these POVs were removed from "Under Pressure." Bowie and Mercury realized they had to cut out the partial, interested eye that desires and speaks only of its personal opinions. The final version also must avail itself of the bird's-eye view of populations in order to become an anthem of broad address and audience.

The whole POV of immersion and reportage of that immersion had to be abandoned. But this didn't necessarily make the eye of biopower — distant, quantifying, and clinical — any more promising as a new form of witnessing in the rock anthem. That is why the song models multiple levels of and forms of street watching. One might be called the POV of the "eyes of love," in tribute to the Edge of Daybreak soul anthem (1979) and in contrast to the "blindness" that "Under Pressure" claims blocks it. But like the perspective of love in "Eyes of Love," this is not a religious or crypto-religious perspective. If the transformation from "Feel Like" to "Under Pressure" is from eros to philia, from one filled with fleshly desire to one of brotherly love, the song contains no agape, love of the divine. The POV of loving the "people on streets" requires human "care" and carries an ethical imperative but not a religious one. It asks one to look on everyone as deserving of the possibility of love and care. But it does so out of no desire for salvation, no appeals to a noumenal realm beyond planetary life. "Under Pressure" still has a place for transcendence, the heightened stakes of melodrama, and its excessive emotional appeals, but of a material and secular kind.

The bodily democracy of Freddie's lust has been abstracted into a POV in which love must be spread to every street in the world, not just the people Bowie and Mercury know personally. The people on the street become objects of love and terror, both forms of care, by the song's end. This is a metaphysics: they are defined as objects of care, candidates for worry and love no matter their personalities, histories, discrete human idiosyncrasies, and singularities.

Love and terror, then, but not pity. The cosmopolitan liberal pity for the "wretched of the earth," found on "We Are the World" and "Do They Know It's Christmas," is missing. Love and terror, unlike liberal pity, require distanced observation and a psychic and emotional feeling of distance between the philanthropist and the sufferer. But what "Under Pressure" argues for is a view of the street in which everyone shares the same fate. Everyone faces the "last dance" found on any street's "edge of the night."

The streets in "Under Pressure" are not exotic tourist destinations; they are home — or, to put it more precisely, they are no less home than anywhere else on this deracinated planet. Requiring no theological apparatus or appeal to a higher power as mediating agent between self and other, what "Under Pressure" posits as a possibility is the street as symbol and location of a shared fragility, the street as the site where we are shorn of myth, shorn of the consoling fiction that some messianic big other will save us from pressure. The *melos* and pathos of the song come from this grounding in the planetary street — its insistence that it is our responsibility to save ourselves.

Now this position has its own ideology, of course. Its vision is classless, raceless, and all but genderless. Everyone on the street should be equal, but of course our world is structurally unequal, riven by class inequality, racism, and patriarchal oppression. Critics have pointed to Bowie's and Queen's riches and fame as disqualifying them from writing a convincing social problem song like "Under Pressure." It's read as evidence of the song being out of touch with the real facts on the ground. After all, it was recorded in Switzerland! By English multimillionaires!

This sort of moralizing about the material situation of creators in relation to their imaginative statements, though, can only go so far. The song makes no bones about the initial differences between people on the street and the singers, implied to be Bowie-like and Mercury-like personas. The universality argued for in the song is one of being subjected to shared danger — pressure is everywhere, and "streets" everywhere share the same problems. It does not make any claims that pressure is equal everywhere, or that Bowie and Mercury understand what it's like to live as subalterns. Universality comes from a negative not a positive force — and it can be experienced differentially while still forming the basis of a sense of shared, planetary danger, which transcends the particular street we live on.

It is easy to misunderstand because so much work influenced by "Under Pressure" misused it to the point of caricature. We've already mentioned the global charity anthems, which allowed us to hear for the first time what it would be like if NGOs had choir. These anthems also strive for universality but assume it as a bland given rather than work to represent it.

In a similar vein, U2's "Where the Streets Have No Name" transcends the streets of Northern Ireland and Ethiopia into the crypto-Christian vision of Bono (future friend of G. W. Bush and Jared Kushner) and turns privation and conflict into optative fusion, a one world united by toxic positivity. Yes, both "Under Pressure" and "Where the Streets Have No Name" feature nameless streets; but only one song is a missionary hymn that ignores the material basis for pain and suffering.

The placeless street, the universal street, then, is necessary to go beyond the narrowness and tribalism of the individual street with its gangs and factions. But it can go either way: toward the universalism of the missionary and the universal blankness of the gentrified system or toward the basis for a future of true democracy in which struggle builds connection.

"Under Pressure" features something that goes beyond what followed and yet also something that lent itself to dreadful influence. Elements that "Under Pressure" keeps in tension were separated out and made the positive "message" of the later songs. And though now most admit that "We Are the World" is cringeworthy, its combination of optimism and pity lives on as one powerful misreading of "Under Pressure."

04 Love and Terror

A WIDESPREAD FEELING OF TERROR, of being terrorized, is a logical outgrowth of a world without a motor (people) for progress (under pressure), without a location from which to act (the street). And terror and the paralysis it subtends have no place in an anthem. An anthem cannot do in a world without an audience to mobilize, a movement to catalyze, and a sense of the scenic and geographic location of this audience and movement.

So terror must be exorcised from "Under Pressure" before the song's end. But unlike previous anthems, the pop anthem of 1981 perhaps could not just ignore the possibility of terror. The world itself was too obtrusively . . . terrorizing. In pop-psychological terms, on "Under Pressure" terror cannot be gone around; it has to be gone through.

No particular nation, community, corporation, or empire could be fixed in order to stop the general crisis. The precarity of life on earth, and the economic and political systems that drove it, seemed out of control, even to individual employees of the most powerful institutions. Things happened to people, almost or wholly unresponsive to human wishes and actions. One could seemingly only watch on in terror, like Bowie's character in "Under Pressure":

> *It's the terror of knowing what this world is about*
> *Watching some good friends screaming "Let me out!"*

The philosophy and theory of the moment were also newly concerned with terror. In a world situation in which contradictions mounted without catharsis, aporias and antinomies continued to pile up like the trash on New York City's streets. Elaine Scarry's *The Body in Pain* and Julia Kristeva's *The Powers of Horror* were both published in this moment and, like "Under Pressure," deal with the problem of a world seemingly united only by a shared sense of pain, trauma, and the sheer fact of having a body open to wounding. Being tortured, for Scarry, and abjection, for Kristeva, are the paradigmatic states of being in the contemporary situation.[1]

In a world in which people, historical progress, and a sense of place have been subtracted, in which community seemed doomed to endless fractalizations, a shared sense of what Theodor Adorno tagged "damaged life" remained a last minimal thread of connection between lonely subjects of postmodernity.[2] We are, often against our will, united only by our pain. Even Fredric Jameson, no trauma theorist, would conclude his introduction to *The Political Unconscious* thus in 1981: "History is what hurts ... refuses desire ... and sets inexorable limits to individual as well as collective practice."[3] This was a very 1981 thing to say. Or as art-punkers Saccharine Trust phrased it on *Paganicons* (also 1981), "Pain is real as real as pain."

The terror in "Under Pressure" is the terror of being powerless before "the suffering of others." Bowie emphasizes the passivity of this terror, and the terror of this passivity, by mismatching one sense, vision (his watching), with the auditory (his "scream"). Now Bowie has long posed as the half-bored flaneur — so this leap into engagement, albeit passive, surprises.

But Bowie's witnessing does not lead his character to intervene directly. It becomes an occasion, rather, to focus on the terror, the passivity that initially strikes the singer, to pause in the terrible knowledge of "what this world is about." This knowledge leads not to a reformist intervention but to frozenness. It would have been maudlin if Bowie's character were to intervene and, say, throw his arm around a suffering "friend" or talk them off the ledge. These characters have been made suicidal by pressure — it would a cheap finale to propose a simple solution to a complex problem.

This encounter, the only remnant of the face-to-face "they're people to me" encounter of the demo, comes with no comforting, ethical quick-fix solution. This is what the world is about, not an aberration or exception but the destructive, annihilatory tendency of historical force on individuals and collectives in post-modernity. The norm of life in the destructive regime of capitalism is the desire to kill yourself: you either participate in the killing of the planet to survive, or you can die by suicide.

Without this grounding knowledge of the song, that it is the world system and not the individual which can be said to possess a death wish, it's easy to misunderstand "Under Pressure" as an ethical song, reducible to bumper-sticker slogans: *Be Kind*, *Unite Against Hate*, *Love Is Love*. If the ground of existence in the song were not established as shifting and lethal, these ethical misreadings might make sense. And of course, it's not wrong to be kind and accepting in your personal life — it's that the structures governing the future of earth's population are so large, complex, and powerful that they are nearly inaccessible to any local application of the golden rule. The pressure is systemic. Yet there is a crack in the system, and this world is not all worlds.

We could say that the *terror of knowing* is a revision of the cosmic horror of earlier Bowie (e.g., "Ashes to Ashes") and the neurasthenic fright of his street witnesses (e.g., "Blackout"). In dialectical fashion, it flows from Bowie's past poses of both cosmic and practical detachment — the scope of the horror remains, as does the flat reportage of outrageous scenes. But the *terror of knowing* the world is both more committed than Bowie's previous detached persona and a rewriting of cosmic loneliness and terror of the screaming abyss into an earthly minded form. It's neither terror embodied nor terror personified, as in goth music (e.g., Bauhaus's "Hollow Hills" and Joy Division's "The Eternal"), as a chthonic malevolence.

It does not attempt to embody the world's abjection all at once or pretend to collapse the difference in position between the sufferer and the observer into a bond of human goodness. Knowledge of terror here functions as empathy and cognition combined — connection between sufferer and witness is not metaphysically impossible, but neither is it the automatic result of human goodness or a clean, empathetic melding of minds and bodies. The terror of knowing is nothing more than a chance for change, no more, no less.

It is much more modest than the sort of radical empathy Scarry believes is possible. When she talks about art in rapturous tones as an agent of repair and healing against the moral stupidity of mind-and-body-destroying torture, she idealistically promotes the aesthetic's powers of reenchantment, à la Kate Bush's in "Cloudbusting": "But just saying it can make it happen." But for Bowie, the *terror of knowing* comes with no guarantee of repair or belief in the power of ethical art to impose a better order onto the material world.

Feeling terror has no essential politics. In 1981, there were no doubt many sources of terror. There's the systematic neglect of the homeless and suicidal of which Bowie and Mercury sing, of course, for starters. And the prospect of a nuclear holocaust looming over everyone's heads was no doubt another contributor to Bowie's terrible knowledge. But the claim of being terrorized or acting on behalf of other's terror could of course be mobilized by reactionaries, and everyone from Ronald Reagan to Bernie Goetz would soon be invoking terror to justify violence in Libya and Nicaragua and on the New York City subway.

This makes the context of Bowie's version of terror important. He's talking about the downtrodden exploited inside a rigged system, one that produces mass suffering to enable the luxury of a few. In this context, terror for Bowie is a feeling that asks for a minimal conceptual recognition: that the world is broken, and we have broken it.

We can position this view on terror and suffering in the modern world against the contemporary ones of Scarry and Kristeva. Kristeva mystifies abjection as a transcendental constant — "I have sought in this book to demonstrate on what mechanism of subjectivity (*which I believe to be universal*) such horror, its meaning as well as its power, is based"— an only nominally historical psychic phenomenon.[4] For her, nothing fundamental can be done for psychic negative states; they are built into what it means to be a human. There is a certain doomer fatalism in her formulations of the abject. She ontologizes terror into an inexorable constant of human existence.

And according to Kristeva, only modernist art, by subverting language and its symbolic codes and engaging, if obliquely, with our psychic fundamentals, can do anything with abjection. At one point, she suggests "a work of disappointment, of frustration, and hollowing" as "probably the only counterweight to abjection."[5] This is settling for mourning over melancholy, depression over sheer horror, a Hobson's choice to be sure. And what art can do is not socially oriented at all — it can only contribute to our knowledge of abjection and the more elusive structures of psychic being.

Like Bowie's knowledge of terror, art can contribute to our knowledge of why we feel abject and terrorized, but it cannot prevent audiences from feeling abjection or heal anyone's psychic trauma. The cold comfort available comes only from analyzing an inexorable problematic, by breaking apart the consolidations of symbolic logic with experimental writing to know (and then only partially) its deeper psychic nature.

But with its emphasis on the unnamable and the irreparable, it could be argued this brand of Lacanian psychoanalysis bears a goth sensibility. In both *The Powers of Horror* and, say, Joy Division's *Closer*, the human animal, with a riven and self-deceiving patchwork of defense mechanisms covering a prelinguistic state of terror, cannot look to institutions, lovers, or friends for succor or safety. The conception of horror in goth and the psychoanalytic theory of the abject in the early eighties is like the titular character in John Carpenter's *The Thing* (1982): a protean spook, irradicable because it thrives parasitically as part of its living host, not as an external "scary monster" but an enemy that is the same shape as its host, and thus inescapable.

Scarry, on the other hand, banks on an ahistorical conception of the healing power of art to "remake" what torture destroys in body and mind. This mystifies the sources of pain and torture as much as Kristeva: if horror is built in to being born of woman in *The Powers of Horror*, so is torture for Scarry in *The Body in Pain*. In pop music, Scarry's vision for non-state healing of the world, the product of a collaboration between the arts and NGOs like Amnesty International, would manifest in songs like "Do They Know It's Christmas" and "We Are the World."

But in "Under Pressure," terror is neither a psychic given nor something redeemable through the speech acts of organizations like Amnesty International or the imaginative sublimity found in the Western canon. For Bowie and Mercury, terror is the feeling of being made to suffer massive damage and accept it as if it were natural: it induces paralysis and extorts quietism from its subject. It is material coercion, not metaphysical curse. It is the *production* of a society that asks us to naturalize trauma as a psychic universal. *This world*, not *all possible worlds*; the world that Bowie and Queen lived in; 1981, not for all time.

In this, the suicide was Bowie's central figure for the place where aesthetic invention and massive psychic damage met. He never broke faith with the modernist conviction that aesthetic and experiential shock were intimately related. And hearing someone screaming "Let me out," witnessing their suffering, was for Bowie a paradigmatic experience of modernity. It was a test of mettle with seemingly no right answers. You can sentimentalize or philosophize the raw suffering of the suicidal, and providing direct aid to the abject often seems impossible.

So the figure of the suicide for Bowie is an incredibly dense nexus of significance. In his music, it's the site where contrarieties intertwine: creative potential and antisocial insanity, personal and public suffering, aesthetics and politics. Even early on with *Ziggy Stardust*'s "Rock 'N' Roll Suicide" (1972), the subject was overladen with so much meaning, the message got lost. While the song's lyrics anticipate R.E.M.'s "Everybody Hurts" and the come-down-from-the-ledge pop subgenre, Bowie's singing is so archly theatrical that it contradicts the assurances his words offer. The suicide is inspiring and terrifying and calls out for impossible help from witnesses.

Bowie's schizophrenic half-brother, Terry Burns, whom he had tried to take in at his Haddon Hall home in the 1970s but had to abandon to Cane Hill Psychiatric Hospital, was suicidal throughout his life. In 1982, he jumped out of a window but survived. In 1985, he died after placing his head on train tracks just outside the asylum. The density of contradictory meanings discussed above were apparent on the rare occasions Bowie discussed Terry:

> One of the times I actually went out with my step-brother [*sic*], I took him to see a Cream concert in Bromley, and about halfway through — and I'd like to think it was during "I Feel Free" — he started feeling very, very bad. And I remember I had to take him out of the club because it was really starting to affect him — he was swaying . . . Anyway, we got out into the street and he collapsed on

the ground and he said the ground was opening up and there was fire and stuff pouring out the pavement, and I could almost see it for him, because he was explaining it so articulately.[6]

This biographical scene comports with the one of terrified spectatorship in "Under Pressure." Here Bowie watches his half-brother suffering an apocalyptic vision, both fascinating and horrifying, just like Kristeva's description of abjection. In both a horrifying and beautiful way, for Bowie the suicide offers proximity to impossible intensity: Blakean visions and limitless suffering, an infinite challenge on the witness to help and a terrifying madness seemingly beyond human aid.

The questions of the genesis, nature, and meaning of contemporary terror were in this sense personal to him. As in "Under Pressure" (which started as a jam on Cream songs including "I Feel Free"), terror is catching, communicable, or at least representable, unlike trauma: "I could almost see it for him," Bowie says. The suffering from schizophrenia of a loved one, watching their terror and "almost seeing it," is a limit case for utopians of the most idealistic cast, at least the ones that believe in the perfectibility of social life through political means.

This is the value of psychoanalysis of Kristeva's type — it insists on not forgetting the loss, damage, pain, confusion, anxiety, horror, and terror that are encountered in life and will not vanish no matter the social dispensation. A highly heritable condition, schizophrenia can sometimes be mitigated but never controlled, perhaps partially managed but not cured. So the temptation is to witness helplessly, to claim that damage and trauma and insanity and suicide will always be with us, despite the political, historical, and social context, and to throw up one's hands.

But this is not Bowie's message in "Under Pressure." For him, terror is a spur to action, if not the solutionism of Scarry's healing arts and "the universal salutation of Amnesty's whispered 'Corragio!'"[7] As with Kristeva and Scarry, Bowie acknowledges the far reach of terror — it knows no boundaries and leads one to think in global terms rather than in discrete domestic units of national and local communities. And the phrase "It's the terror of knowing what this world is about" is seemingly as much a blanket claim as Kristeva's about the ontological existence of horror or Scarry's that the dance shared by torture and healing has persisted since the days of "Isaiah's ancient artisans."[8]

The usage of terror in "Under Pressure" disrupts both Kristeva's fatalism and Scarry's voluntarism. One gloss of Bowie's "terror of knowing" might be that it asks for action with full recognition of how little the individual can do to affect worldwide change. By combining Kristeva's dark knowledge with Scarry's recognition that contemplation is not enough, Bowie goes beyond them both. Unlike *Power of Horror* or *Body in Pain*, "Under Pressure" never seems merely pessimistic or optimistic, because it asks the listener to deal with what is and work toward what should be, without hope of success.

What's more, the pleasure terror indecently imparts, which commentators from Aristotle to Edmund Burke to Saidiya Hartman have noted, means a natural outpouring of benevolence toward sufferers cannot be depended on. This is why the "knowing" part of Bowie's phrase "the terror of knowing what this world is about," the intellectual part of witnessing, is so important. Here Bowie complicates the scene of terror with a logical dimension as well as an affective one. One feels all sorts of things when confronted with raw, spontaneous, and sudden events of a shocking nature: a jumble of confused terror, joy, gloom, and excitement. We don't always react in accordance with our ethical precepts. Bowie's knowing forces reflection into the scene of witnessing — it cannot be all gut reaction, because we will not automatically identify with a victim, target, or sufferer of violence and oppression. In "Under Pressure," care is also a process of apprehension, a processing of raw and immediate bodily reaction.

Raw reactions within a society that conditions one to so much cruelty are bound to themselves often be cruel, or at least mix desire and pleasure with the sight and sounds of the pain of others. Fascism and all other forms of political terror, of course, depend on visceral reactions that short-circuit reflection, consideration, and analysis. They are the politics of the snap judgment. Within the welter of emotion, often confused and self-contradictory, Bowie insists on thought, connecting the impulses of the moment with an understanding of its historical situation. Rather than propagandizing for specific humanitarian interventions or sketching the limits of our psychic powerlessness, Bowie models a general way to feel, think, and (ultimately) act in response to structural victimization, which we call life on earth under capitalism.

But knowing for Bowie is not the final stage of an encounter with another's victimization. To be terrorized, to feel torn by identification, sympathy, and, yes, a certain quantum of pleasure, and then grapple with those feelings — all these are just preliminaries.

Most academics leave the argument here. Critical analysis thrives in the negative mode; it unlooses the strands of texts, historical events, and political ideologies to demystify. But Bowie's call to practice does something few scholars have ever managed to do believably: end with an exhortation to live, think, and act differently that *feels* convincing.

Bowie and Mercury ask us not just to feel terror, or to understand terror's function in the modern world, but also, after we have, to do something about it. And while songs are symbolic, they also *move people*: as Shana Redmond put it, "anthems require subscription to a system of beliefs that stir and organize the receivers of the music."[9] What's the last book of theory that moved you? Bowie and Mercury's "Under Pressure" embodies the world's need for love; it doesn't merely cite it. And that's ultimately why people still care about the song. It's the visceral, heightened emotional stakes of the song, its desire to draw out melodramatic, physical reactions, that caused Thom Yorke of Radiohead to use it as his example of the "ideal pop song": "Songs like 'Under Pressure,' something that *makes you want to fall down on your knees.*"[10] By working through the complications of its historical moment — the terror, death, delusion, and confusion that characterized neoliberalism ascendant — "Under Pressure" earns the ability to convincingly provide a glimpse of an alternative. Love, not in the form of a Hallmark card or a faded Day-Glo bumper sticker, but as a difficult practice with no guarantees of success.

This is fitting because, since 1945, pop music has taken possession of love. Not poetry, not philosophy, not even French film has had the power to reinvent love in hearts and minds that popular music has and continues to possess. But if love was the answer to civilizational crisis in the late sixties of Wilhelm Reich and Herbert Marcuse, by the time of "Under Pressure" things were not so simple. By 1976, Foucault was already arguing that love and desire could and have been a sneaky lever for social control: by manufacturing our identities for us, and so the limits of our political theory and practice, love keeps us domesticated. For Foucault, the contemporary erotics Queen toyed with in "Crazy Little Thing Called Love" (1979) and Bowie lightly skewered in "Modern Love" (1983) were far from a straightforward force for revolution and liberation.

According to Foucault, the obsession with sexual identity, as the essential basis for our political and philosophical truth, was as much a constraint on radical social transformation as a source of future liberation. In 1977, Roland Barthes was complaining that everywhere "the most divergent systems" were being invoked to "demystify, to limit, to erase, in short to depreciate love."[11] By 1986, Jean-Luc Nancy was wondering "has not everything been said on the subject of love? Every excess and every exactitude?"[12] Love was paradoxically everywhere but cheapened, perhaps even void of meaning entirely.

If love was no longer all we needed, all there is, and/or the conqueror of all, what was it? Pop anthemicists (and filmmakers) and French theorists seemed to be the only ones still seeking a serious (or frivolous, as the case may be) answer to the question. Whether it was exiled (Barthes) or exhausted (Nancy) or politically complicit with social control (Foucault), it appeared (to male French theorists, a darkened glass surely but a mirror of the times nonetheless) love no longer spoke or lived for desire, joy, or possibility. Left to its own devices, without a countermovement, whether it be emotional rescue (Barthes), conceptual shoring up through ontology (Nancy and later Alain Badiou), or micropolitical experimentation (Foucault, Deleuze), love and desire seemed doomed to become an embarrassment — either as a symbol of the political naivete of the 1960s, as an aesthetic nightmare of melodrama and sentimentality, as an engine of social reproduction, or as a secret sharer in our own self-policing.

Like love, the anthem (and above all the love anthem) was in 1981 newly embarrassing. Love needed to be reinvented and reapplied, and even pop musicians agreed. There was something suspect about taking love as a theme in contemporary life. As Queen bassist Roger Taylor relayed in 1982, "Everybody laughed when they asked what 'Under Pressure' was all about. It's quite simply about love, which is the most un-cool, un-hip thing."[13] Yet in the twentieth century, pop music owned love — even if it was abandoned, exhausted, or discredited, it was built into pop's form and content. It couldn't be tossed aside for pastiche, angst, rage, or abstraction. What, besides perhaps the cinema, has dominated the theory and practice of love more than pop music?

French theory, and philosophy in general from Plato and Søren Kierkegaard through, certainly paled in comparison and is more useful as an x-ray of the time than as an agent of change in the moment. Nothing in it had the productive power to reshape subjectivity, change minds, and introduce new forms of amatory relation than the love song in the twentieth century. And as a new sound media, it reached into bodies and souls while maintaining a link with both the metrics and physicality of poetics and the capabilities of representation of narrative.

As a media, it was more immediate than poetry and narrative, whose functions it subsumed; as an aesthetic form, it took up the contemporary meaning of love as one of its primary preoccupations, throughout its many genres, modes, trends, and fads. The fact that popular music repeatedly fails to show up in theory, including theory on love, or appears in a clichéd presentation, continues to be a missed opportunity for criticism.

But by 1981, love needed to become "modern" for the pop anthem, too. As with the French theorists, the old forms neither represented contemporary love nor opened up a place for its transformative power in the new world. Young love, free love, militant love, hedonistic love, doomed love had all soured as forces with real power behind them in the modern world. Countermovements based on an ethos of love were easily exhausted and broken up, while the institutional and corporate machinery of the 1970s and 1980s proved increasingly capable of capturing, colonizing, and marketing coupling and love, sex and desire. These last were more generally as reactionary compensations for a lack of larger political, collective, and global horizons of joy, liberation, and justice.

But in the latter half of the seventies, disco carried the mantle for a new thematic of love. As detailed in Tim Lawrence's *Love Saves the Day*, figures like David Mancuso functioned as the bridge from sixties perceptual experimentation with sex and drugs to the dance culture of the seventies.[14] Disco and its inheritors hi-NRG, boogie, house, and techno all allowed minor utopias to be carved out in clubs, basements, garages, warehouses, small studios, bathhouses, radio stations, and even occasionally record pools. These were, at least in the ideal shape as embodied in the dance music of groups from the space disco of Cloud One to the love house of Ten City, spaces of love, an antinormative love that linked together outsiders, outcasts, and countercultural habitués in resistance and counterhegemonic example to the hostility, competition, and violence dominating the legal and criminal worlds alike. Here, love was celebrated not as a means to universal liberation but as something more along the lines of

Foucault's exploration of the reinvention of desire, a counternormative *ars erotica*, and pleasure was the means to new identities and social relations within smaller groups necessarily positioned in opposition to normal, mainstream popular culture.

"Under Pressure" is finally maximalist on love. Unlike disco (Mancuso's not Rick Dees's), it refuses to tarry at the subcultural level or identify itself straightforwardly with erotic transgression of moral norms. Rather, as an anthem, it seems to name and articulate the many types of modern love and address *everyone* through that articulation. By doing so, it keeps faith with the universalist ambition of the older anthems while accounting for the manifold varieties of its particular forms.

This is where the dialogical, combative power of the duet form becomes so important. In "Under Pressure," two forms of love are offered and ultimately intertwined. Freddie Mercury offers a familiar utopian vision: a world united by epiphanic, collective sensuality. In keeping with the sixties flavor of this sentiment, love (like peace for the Beatles) must be given "that one more chance." But for David Bowie, love is something that must be given not simply a chance but a "dare." The slight difference is significant. For Mercury, love is a free choice, a chance taken to revel in the natural equality of bodies; for Bowie, it's a dare, a call from a world under heavy pressure. It is a risky *demand* from a bleeding, burning planet. You can refuse such a dare, but it won't get you out of suffering the consequences of your refusal. Mercury, on the hand, begins speaking the language of ABBA's recent hit "Take a Chance On Me" (1977): a song of zipless erotics and bodily democracy.

Bowie reframes Mercury's aleatoric, sensual form of loving into a political decision exacted by the material world — suffering is asking you to take a side, and you will be judged depending on which side of love you fall. Bowie's love asks for a more specific commitment than Mercury's: it asks you to care for "people on the edge of the night," to include society's excluded, damaged, troubled, and discarded. The people on the edge of the night are all those who cannot be counted for in the present political dispensation.

This call, to go beyond the lines and limits drawn by the current system, falls in the lap of the listener at the song's end, but not before another shade of meaning for love is thrown into the mix. Because love also, Bowie informs us, "dares you to change our way of caring about ourselves." The full inclusion of "people on the edge of the night" into one's care also requires "caring about ourselves." This form of self-care, unlike the prevailing antisocial one of today, includes a belief in the priorness of the collective to the individual. In "Under Pressure," you can only care for yourself if you care about "ourselves." In other words, we can achieve genuine self-love only if we envision ourselves as part of a community that grants full equality to even those hitherto uncounted.

Finally, the stakes are heightened one more time by Bowie's next announcement, that "this is our last dance." This concluding image of the last dance allows all the song's senses of love to register at once: the last dance of Bowie and Mercury as duet partners, the last dance of a romantic couple, the dance of the haves and the have-nots, spectators and sufferers, and the last dance of us all on a planet that is in these last lines revealed to be caught in its end-times. All the levels of love and care in the song whirl around the stage in this last dance: the erotic, the ethical, the political, and even, surprisingly, the apocalyptic world-historical.

Like all the best pop anthems, "Under Pressure" allows the additive, dream logic of multiple truths to accumulate — it provides access to a fantasy world in which multiple forms of love, perhaps mutually exclusive in the real world, can strengthen one another in the dreaming listener. Mercury and Bowie's vision of love during this last dance, then, asks for loving commitment to the world at all of its overlapping levels: of the lover, the witness, the citizen, the worker, and the earthling.

In "Under Pressure," the stakes of answering the call of love are melodramatically world-historical because the alternative is apocalypse. An immodest pop anthem, "Under Pressure" stops at the very limits of its form — the point where it demands actual transformation in the material world. Beyond this point, a pop anthem cannot go: the song asks its listeners to finish its work and make its fantasy real.

ACKNOWLEDGMENTS

Nathan Bowles, Dylan Brzezinski, Joe Brzezinski, Malcolm Brzezinski, Mary Brzezinski, Joshua Clover, Nihad Farooq, Jake X. Fussell, Barbie Halaby, Sarah Harlan, Nathan Hensley, Bill Knight, Lisa Lawley, Emily Lordi, Kate Mullen, Katie O'Neil, Chris Robinson, Nate Smith, Ken Wissoker, and the two anonymous reviewers for Duke University Press.

NOTES

Lyrics, unless otherwise noted, are the author's transcription.

Introduction

1. Horid, "Queen Deserves."

2. May, "Queen Guitarist Brian May."

3. Benitez-Eves, "Roger Taylor"; Jones, *Mercury*, 194.

4. Thompson, "Liner Notes."

5. James, *Black Jacobins*, 317–18.

6. Hobsbawm, *Age of Extremes*, chap. 14.

7. Deleuze and Guattari, *What Is Philosophy?*, 175.

8. Reggio, *Koyaanisqatsi*.

9. D'Adamo, "Ain't There One Damn Flag," 126, 140.

10. Donald Fagen, quoted in Borrelli, "Steely Dan Singer."

11. Haden, back cover notes.

12. Gilroy, *"There Ain't No Black."*

13. Bangs, "James Taylor Marked," 61–62.

14. Freddie Mercury, quoted in Clerc, *Queen All the Songs*, 55.

15. Fredric Jameson, quoted in Baumbach, Young, and Yue, "Revisiting Postmodernism," 144; italics mine.

16. Matos, *Can't Slow Down*, 3.

17. Deleuze and Parnet, *Dialogues II*, 48.

18. Blake, *Is This the Real Life?*, 258.

19. Raggett, "Under Pressure."

20. O'Leary, *Ashes to Ashes*, 170.

21. O'Leary, *Ashes to Ashes*, 168.

22. Gates, "Bill Gates's Desert Island."

23. Pegg, *Complete David Bowie*, 241; May, "Exclusive."

Chapter 1. Pressure

1. *Oxford English Dictionary*, s.v. "Pressure."

2. Bowie had probably heard "Pressure Drop" performed live at the Montreux Jazz Festival in July 1981, immediately before recording "Under Pressure."

3. *Far Out Magazine*, "Story Behind."

4. *Far Out Magazine*, "Story Behind."

5. Parker, "Brian May."

6. Little Richard, "1972."

7. Foucault, *Security, Territory, Population*, 105; Deleuze, "Postscript," 4.

8. O'Leary, *Ashes to Ashes*, 170.

9. Badiou, "Bourgeois Right."

Chapter 2. People

1. Mr. Mixx, "2 Live Crew's DJ."

2. Charles Hayward, quoted in Calvert, "Final Warning."

3. Michael Hampton, quoted in Simpson, "How We Made."

4. Foucault, "Omnes et Singulatim."

5. Keats, *Letters*, 101–2.

6. Jakobson, "Shifters," 132.

7. Bowie, "Molly Meldrum Interviews David Bowie."

8. Bowie, "Interview with David Bowie."

Chapter 3. Streets

1. Simmel, "Metropolis and Mental Life."

2. Ehrenreich, *Dancing in the Streets*.

3. Jackson, *Freddie Mercury*, chap. 16.

4. Joyce, *Ulysses*, 368.

5. Gibson, "Burning Chrome," 106.

6. Harvey, *Spaces of Hope*.

7. Hall, *Policing the Crisis*, 394.

Chapter 4. Love and Terror

1. Scarry, *Body in Pain*; Kristeva, *Powers of Horror*.

2. Adorno, *Minima Moralia*.

3. Jameson, *Political Unconscious*, 102.

4. Kristeva, *Powers of Horror*, 208 (italics mine).

5. Kristeva, *Powers of Horror*, 220.

6. Bowie and Anderson, "Bowie and Brett."

7. Scarry, *Body in Pain*, 326.

8. Scarry, *Body in Pain*, 326.

9. Redmond, *Anthem*, 3.

10. Schneider, "Radiohead's Thom Yorke" (italics mine).

11. Barthes, *Lover's Discourse*, 22.

12. Nancy, *Inoperative Community*, 82.

13. Greenleaf and Hyman, "Queen on the Road."

14. Lawrence, *Love Saves the Day*.

BIBLIOGRAPHY

Adorno, Theodor W. *Minima Moralia: Reflections from Damaged Life*. Translated by E. F. N. Jephcott. New York: Verso, 2018.

Badiou, Alain. "We Have to Break Bourgeois Right." Translated by David Fernbach. *Verso Books* (blog), August 12, 2020. https://www .versobooks.com/blogs/news/4819-we-have -to-break-bourgeois-right.

Bangs, Lester. "James Taylor Marked for Death." In Lester Bangs, *Psychotic Reactions and Carburetor Dung*, edited by Greil Marcus, 53–81. New York: Anchor Books, 1987.

Barthes, Roland. *A Lover's Discourse: Fragments*. Translated by Richard Howard. New York: Hill and Wang, 1978.

Baumbach, Nico, Damon R. Young, and Genevieve Yue. "Revisiting Postmodernism: An Interview with Fredric Jameson." *Social Text* 34, no. 2 (127) (2016): 143–60.

Benitez-Eves, Tina. "Roger Taylor Releases First Solo Album in Eight Years." *American Songwriter*, 2021. https://americansong writer.com/roger-taylor-releases-first -solo-album-in-eight-years/.

Blake, Mark. *Is This the Real Life?* New York: Da Capo, 2011.

Borrelli, Christopher. "Steely Dan Singer Donald Fagen Just 'Being Honest' in New Book." *Chicago Tribune*, October 23, 2013.

Bowie, David. "David Bowie." Interview by Mavis Nicholson. *Afternoon Plus*, Thames Television, February 2, 1979. https://www .youtube.com/watch?v=LwTFW4kfHl4.

Bowie, David. "Molly Meldrum Interviews David Bowie." Australian Broadcasting Corporation, *Countdown*, March 1983. YouTube video. https://www.youtube.com /watch?v=Ll5njWPdjoY.

Bowie, David, and Brett Anderson. "Bowie and Brett Alias Smith and Jones (Part Two)." Interview by Steve Sutherland. *NME*, March 27, 1993. https://bowieandbrett.wordpress.com /2016/01/13/bowie-and-brett-alias-smith -and-jones-part-two-nme-27-march-1993/.

Calvert, John. "The Final Warning: Three Decades after This Heat's *Deceit*." *The Quietus*, June 7, 2011.

Clerc, Benoît. *Queen: All the Songs — The Story Behind Every Track*. New York: Running Press, 2020.

Critchley, Simon. *Bowie*. New York: OR Books, 2016.

D'Adamo, Amedeo. "Ain't There One Damn Flag That Can Make Me Break Down and Cry?: The Formal, Performative and Emotional Tactics of Bowie's Singular Critical Anthem 'Young Americans.'" In *Enchanting David Bowie: Space/Time/Body/Memory*, edited by Toija Cinque, Christopher Moore, and Sean Redmond, 119 – 52. London: Bloomsbury Academic, 2015.

Deleuze, Gilles. "Postscript on the Societies of Control." *October* 59 (1992): 3 – 7. http://www.jstor.org/stable/778828.

Deleuze, Gilles, and Félix Guattari. *What Is Philosophy?* Translated by Hugh Tomlinson. New York: Columbia University Press, 1996.

Deleuze, Gilles, and Claire Parnet. *Dialogues II*. New York: Columbia University Press, 2002.

Ehrenreich, Barbara. *Dancing in the Streets: A History of Collective Joy*. New York: Henry Holt, 2006.

Far Out Magazine. "The Story Behind the Song: David Bowie and Queen's Cocaine-Fuelled Romp 'Under Pressure.'" October 27, 2021. https://faroutmagazine.co.uk/david-bowie-queen-freddie-mercury-under-pressure-story-1981/.

Foucault, Michel. "Omnes et Singulatim: Towards a Criticism of Political Reason." In *The Tanner Lectures on Human Values 1981*, edited by Sterling M. McMurrin, 2:225 – 54. Salt Lake City: University of Utah Press, 1981.

Foucault, Michel. *Security, Territory, Population: Lectures at the Collège de France 1977 – 1978*. Translated by Graham Burchell. New York: Picador, 2009.

Gates, Bill. "Bill Gates's Desert Island Playlist." Interview by Kirsty Young. *BBC News*, January 31, 2016. https://www.bbc.com/news/magazine-35442969.

Gibson, William. "Burning Chrome." *Omni* 46 (July 1982): 72 – 107.

Gilroy, Paul. *"There Ain't No Black in the Union Jack": The Cultural Politics of Race and Nation*. Chicago: University of Chicago Press, 1991.

Greenleaf, Vicki, and Stan Hyman. "Queen on the Road Again." *International Musician and Recording World*, November 1982.

Haden, Charlie. Back cover notes for Charlie Haden, *Liberation Music Orchestra*. Santa Monica, CA: Impulse! AS-9183, 1970. LP.

Hall, Stuart. *Policing the Crisis*. London: Macmillan, 1978.

Harvey, David. *Spaces of Hope*. Edinburgh: Edinburgh University Press, 2002.

Hobsbawm, Eric. *Age of Extremes: The Short Twentieth Century, 1914 – 1991*. New York: Vintage, 1996.

Horid, Rosy. "Queen Deserves Rock's Royal Crown?" *Circus*, January 19, 1978.

Jackson, Laura. *Freddie Mercury: The Biography*. Rev. ed. London: Piatkus, 2011.

Jakobson, Roman. "Shifters, Verbal Categories, and the Russian Verb." In *Selected Writings*, 2:130 – 47. The Hague: Mouton, 1971.

James, C. L. R. *The Black Jacobins*. 2nd ed. New York: Vintage Books, 1989.

Jameson, Fredric. *The Political Unconscious*. Ithaca, NY: Cornell University Press, 1981.

Jones, Lesley-Ann. *Mercury: An Intimate Biography of Freddie Mercury*. London: Hodder and Stoughton, 2011.

Joyce, James. *Ulysses*. Edited by Hans Walter Gabler, Wolfhard Steppe, and Claus Melchior. New York: Vintage, 1986.

Keats, John. *The Letters of John Keats*. Edited by Hyder E. Rollins. 2 vols. Cambridge, MA: Harvard University Press, 1958.

Kristeva, Julia. *Powers of Horror: An Essay on Abjection*. Translated by Leon Roudiez. New York: Columbia University Press, 1984.

Lawrence, Tim. *Love Saves the Day: A History of American Dance Music Culture, 1970 – 1979*. Durham, NC: Duke University Press, 2003.

Little Richard. "1972: Little Richard Interview Is the GOAT." Interview by Ray Connolly. bbc Archive, *Late Night Line-Up*, August 4, 1972. YouTube video. https://www.youtube.com/watch?v=Btdzp52AmsE.

Matos, Michaelangelo. *Can't Slow Down: How 1984 Became Pop's Blockbuster Year*. New York: Hachette, 2020.

May, Brian. "Exclusive: Brian May Tells How Bowie and Queen Wrote the Legendary Track Under Pressure." *Daily Mirror*, January 11, 2016.

May, Brian. "Fresh Air's Summer Music Interviews: Queen Guitarist Brian May." Interview by Terry Gross. NPR, *Fresh Air*, August 29, 2022. https://www.npr.org/2022/08/29/1119640665/fresh-airs-summer-music-interviews-queen-guitarist-brian-may.

Mr. Mixx. "2 Live Crew's DJ and Producer Mr. Mixx on the Roots of Miami Bass." Interview by Jesse Serwer. *Red Bull Music Academy*, July 7, 2016. https://daily.redbullmusicacademy.com/2016/07/mr-mixx-interview.

Nancy, Jean-Luc. *The Inoperative Community*. Minneapolis: University of Minnesota Press, 1991.

O'Leary, Chris. *Ashes to Ashes: The Songs of David Bowie, 1976 – 2016*. New York: Repeater Books, 2019.

Oxford English Dictionary. 2nd ed. Oxford: Oxford University Press, 1989.

Parker, Matt. "Brian May Says David Bowie Removed His Electric Guitar Riffs on Under Pressure — And He Never Liked The Results." *Guitar World,* February 12, 2024. https://www.guitarworld.com/news/brian-may-under-pressure-riff-david-bowie-mix.

Pegg, Nicholas. *The Complete David Bowie*. London: Reynolds and Hearn, 2009.

Raggett, Ned. "Under Pressure": David Bowie/Queen track notes. AllMusic, accessed May 7, 2024. https://www.allmusic.com/song/under-pressure-mt0044908466.

Redmond, Shana L. *Anthem: Social Movements and the Sound of Solidarity in the African Diaspora*. New York: NYU Press, 2014.

Reggio, Godfrey, dir. *Koyaanisqatsi*. San Francisco: American Zoetrope, 1982.

Scarry, Elaine. *The Body in Pain*. New York: Oxford University Press, 1985.

Schneider, Martin. "Radiohead's Thom Yorke in 1993: Bowie and Queen's 'Under Pressure' Is the Perfect Pop Song." Dangerous Minds, February 22, 2017. https://dangerousminds.net/comments/radioheads_thom_yorke_in_1993_bowie_and_queens_under_pressure.

Simmel, Georg. "The Metropolis and Mental Life." In *The Sociology of Georg Simmel*, edited by K. H. Wolff, 409 – 24. New York: The Free Press, 1950.

Simpson, Dave. "How We Made Funkadelic's *One Nation Under a Groove*." *Guardian*, June 4, 2018.

Thompson, Mayo. Liner notes for the Red Crayola with Art & Language, *Kangaroo?* Rough Trade 19, 1981.

Waldrep, Shelton. *Future Nostalgia: Performing David Bowie*. London: Bloomsbury Academic, 2016.

INDEX